Capturing Moments: 52 Inspirational Photography Ideas

Unlock Your Creative Potential with Superb Subject Suggestions, Comprehensive Tips, Tricks, Techniques, and Camera Settings

Gary Hulland

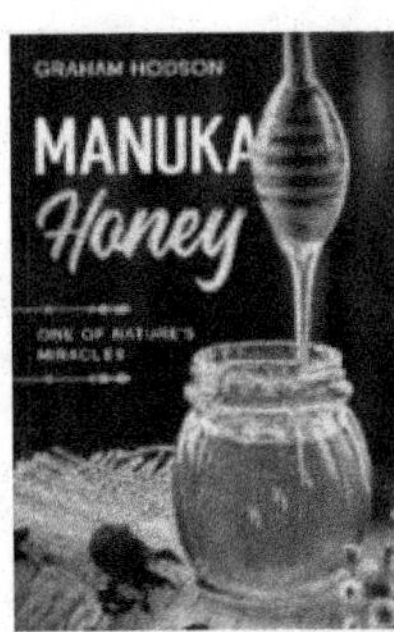

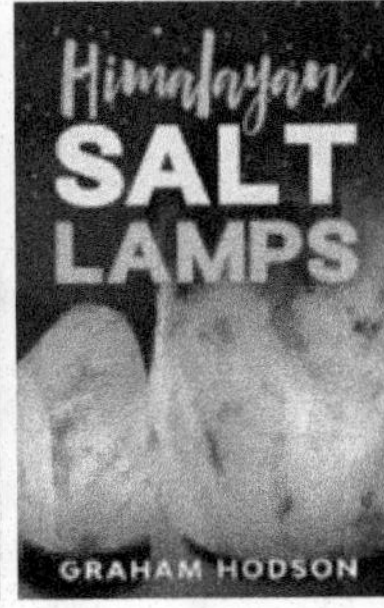

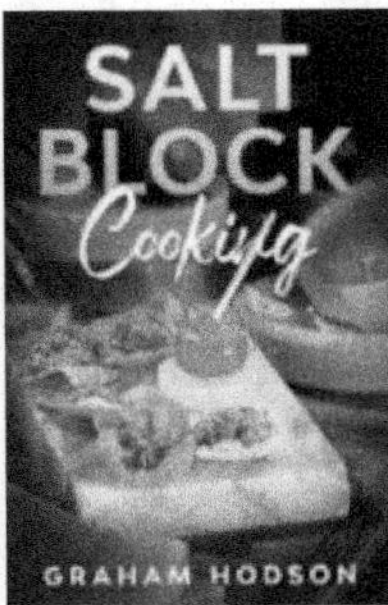

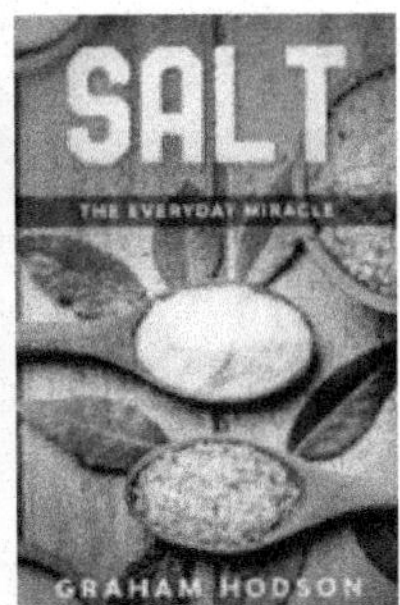

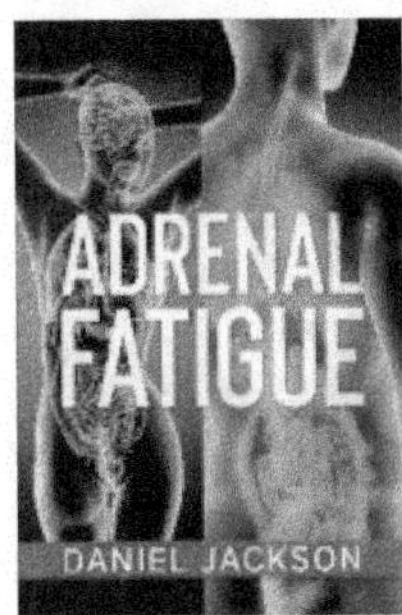

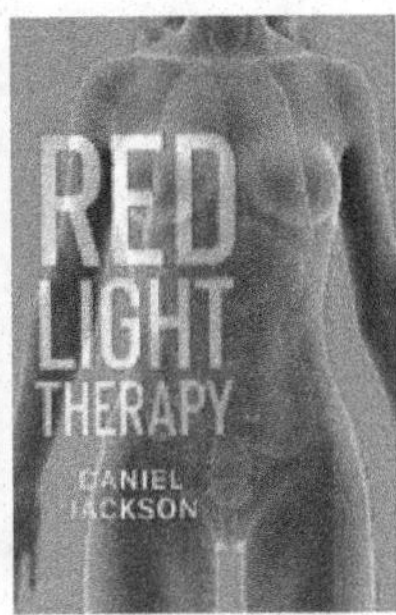

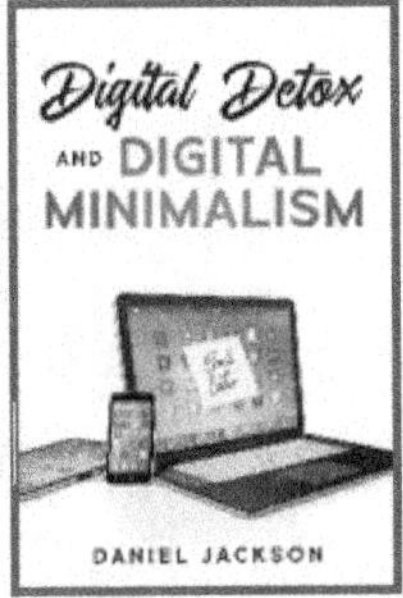

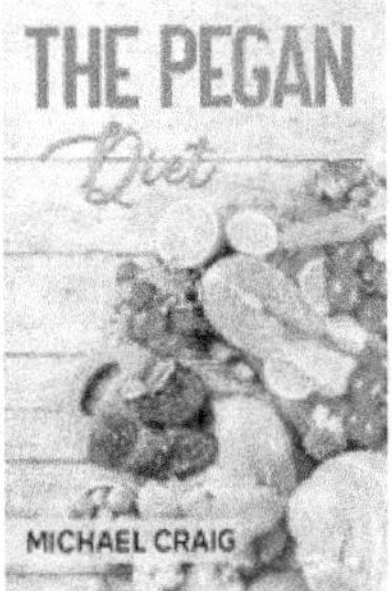

Take a look at more great books available from Rockwood Publishing

... some for FREE!

Just visit the link below:

rockwoodpublishing.co.uk

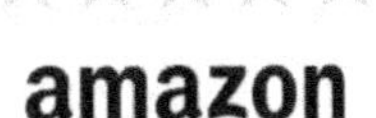
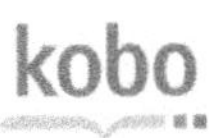
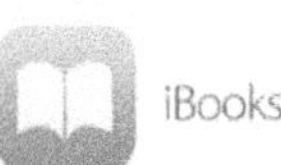
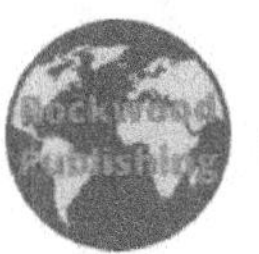
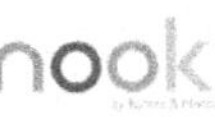
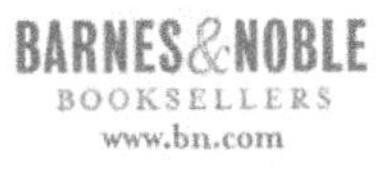

Contents

52 Fabulous Photography Ideas
– At A Glance

1. A beautiful sunrise or sunset
2. A city skyline at night
3. A local landmark or historical monument
4. A close-up of a colorful flower
5. An interesting street scene
6. A dramatic weather event (e.g., storm clouds, lightning)
7. A stunning natural landscape
8. A group of friends or family members
9. A candid moment between people
10. A unique architectural detail
11. Street art or graffiti
12. A pet or interesting animal
13. A long-exposure image of traffic
14. A macro shot of an insect or small creature
15. A reflection in water or a mirror
16. A silhouette against a vibrant background
17. A high-contrast black and white image
18. A delicious meal or food item
19. A busy market or shopping area
20. A serene waterscape (e.g., lake, river, ocean)
21. An amusement park or carnival
22. A sporting event or action shot
23. A local festival or cultural event
24. A captivating portrait
25. A bird in flight or perched
26. A bustling city street
27. A starry night sky or astrophotography
28. A seasonal change (e.g., autumn leaves, snowfall)

29.   A long shadow cast by a person or object

30.   A rainbow or other atmospheric phenomenon

31.   A still life of everyday objects

32.   A macro shot of a water droplet or dew

33.   A local artisan at work (e.g., glassblower, barista, blacksmith)

34.   A panoramic view

35.   A piece of abstract art

36.   A vibrant sunset or sunrise through trees

37.   A spiral staircase or unique architectural element

38.   A musical performance or musician

39.   A dancer or other performing artist

40.   A colorful door or window

41.   A busy airport or train station

42.   A public garden or park

43.   A person engaged in their hobby or craft

44.   A neon sign or interesting light source

45.   A vintage car or mode of transportation

46.   A foggy or misty scene

47.   An interesting pattern or texture

48.   A time-lapse of a busy area

49.   A romantic scene

50.   An abandoned building or urban exploration

51.   A unique sculpture or installation art

52.   A moment of joy or laughter

Introduction

A Year of Visual Magic

Welcome, fellow shutterbugs and aspiring photographers, to a thrilling journey through the world of photography! If you're holding this book in your hands or scrolling through it on your digital device, congratulations! You've taken the first step toward capturing 52 weeks of pure visual magic.

Whether you're a seasoned pro, a hobbyist with a keen eye, or an absolute beginner with nothing more than a smartphone, you're in for a treat.

This book is designed to inspire, teach, and challenge you, all while filling your life with creativity and joy. So buckle up, strap on your camera bag, and get ready to explore the wonderful world of photography.

Each week, you'll be presented with a fresh, unique idea for something to photograph. We'll guide you through the process, offering helpful tips, tricks, and techniques to make your photos truly shine.

You'll learn about composition, lighting, perspective, and storytelling, all while discovering new subjects and expanding your photographic horizons.

Throughout the pages of this book, you'll find a delightful mix of the expected and the unexpected. Some weeks, you'll be capturing the beauty of a golden sunrise or the vibrant colors of a bustling cityscape.

Other weeks, you'll be diving into the abstract, snapping photos of reflections or exploring the intricate details of everyday objects. And for those feeling particularly adventurous, there will be challenges that will push you to experiment and think outside the box (or viewfinder).

The beauty of this book is that you can follow the 52 ideas in order, or you can flip to a random page and let serendipity guide your photographic journey. There's no right or wrong way to approach this adventure; the only requirement is a willingness to learn, grow, and have fun!

As you progress through the weeks, you'll find that photography is more than just the art of taking pictures. It's a way of life, a way of seeing the world, and a way of telling stories without uttering a single word.

You'll learn to appreciate the subtle nuances of light and shadow, the intricate patterns of nature, and the fleeting moments of emotion that make life so rich and beautiful.

But, don't be fooled: as much as we'd love to say it's all rainbows and perfectly focused butterflies, photography can also be frustrating at times. There will be days when the lighting just won't cooperate or when you can't quite capture the image you had in mind.
But remember, every great photographer has faced these challenges and has come out the other side stronger and

more skilled. Keep practicing, experimenting, and above all, have fun. After all, the best photographs are often born from happy accidents and unexpected surprises.

So, as you embark on this year-long journey, remember that photography is not a destination, but a continuous process of discovery and growth. Embrace the ups and downs, and find joy in the smallest victories. And, above all, never forget the wise words of renowned photographer Ansel Adams: "You don't take a photograph, you make it."

Now, without further ado, let's dive into the first of your 52 great ideas for things to photograph. The world is your canvas, and your camera is your paintbrush. So, grab your gear, open your eyes, and let the adventure begin!

Please remember that the most important aspect of photography is to have fun and experiment with different subjects, perspectives, and techniques.

Let your creativity and personal interests guide you in capturing images that truly resonate with you.

Happy snapping!

I pondered long and hard as to whether or not to put examples of photographs in this book because to some people a book about photography with no photographs could seem a little strange.

However, in the end, it was quite an easy decision to make for the simple reason that including example images would be the very opposite of what I was trying to achieve with the book in the first place, and that is... *the fundamental importance of individuality.*

I didn't want to run the risk of there being any "A/B" comparisons or "Oh, that's not as good as the one in the book". Absolutely not! That would go against everything I hold dear about photography.

When you're out there using this book to help you create fabulous photographs...

- **This is YOUR moment, not somebody else's.**
- **There should be no comparing "yours to theirs".**
- **There is no right or wrong, just what YOU come up with.**
- **This is your vision, your effort, your art.**

Enjoy!

1. A beautiful sunrise or sunset

Capturing the Magic of Sunrises and Sunsets: A Photographer's Ode to Nature's Masterpiece

Ah, sunrises and sunsets! The universe's daily reminder that beauty exists in fleeting moments, and that endings can be just as beautiful as beginnings.

As a photography enthusiast, I can't help but be captivated by the allure of these natural spectacles. Allow me to take you on a journey to explore the art of capturing sunrises and sunsets, igniting your passion and inspiring your inner artist.

First, let's talk timing. You know what they say, "The early bird gets the worm," or in this case, "The early photographer captures the stunning sunrise." Arriving early to scout your location and prepare your equipment is key. Remember, the sun waits for no one – except maybe in the Arctic, where it takes its sweet time rising and setting, but I digress.

Composition is crucial when photographing sunrises and sunsets. Rule of thirds? More like the rule of awes! Placing the horizon on the top or bottom third of your frame adds visual interest and showcases the sky's dramatic hues.

You can also experiment with silhouettes to create striking contrasts between the warm tones of the sky and the mysterious shadows of the foreground.

The world is your canvas, so paint with the light and create your masterpiece.

Let's talk settings, and I don't mean the ones on your dinner table. When capturing these magical moments, you'll want to play around with your camera's manual mode.

Aperture, shutter speed, and ISO are the Holy Trinity of photography, and finding the right balance will help you achieve that perfect shot.

Remember, photography is all about experimentation; much like trying to fold a fitted sheet, it may take a few attempts before you nail it.
Don't be afraid to harness the power of filters.

Graduated neutral density filters can be your best friend when tackling the dynamic range of a vibrant sky. Think of them as sunglasses for your camera, helping to keep those pesky overexposed highlights in check, while allowing the shadows to sing their melodious tune.

Never underestimate the importance of post-processing. Just like a pinch of salt can elevate a dish, a few adjustments in Lightroom or Photoshop can transform your image from "meh" to "magnificent." But be cautious not to overdo it, as you don't want your photo to resemble a unicorn's daydream.

Now, let's address the elephant in the room, or rather, the smartphone in your pocket. Yes, you can capture breathtaking sunrises and sunsets with your trusty phone camera. With the right composition, a dash of creativity, and a sprinkle of editing apps, you can create a visual feast worthy of any social media platform.

In conclusion, photographing sunrises and sunsets is a transcendent experience that allows us to appreciate the beauty and wonder of our world. It's an opportunity to slow down, connect with nature, and create lasting memories through our art. So, grab your camera, head outdoors, and seize the day (or the twilight) – after all, you know what they say, "Red sky at night, photographer's delight; red sky in the morning, photographer's warning." Just kidding, there's no such saying, but maybe there should be! Happy shooting!

Camera settings

Capturing the perfect sunrise or sunset photo often requires a combination of the right camera settings and some experimentation.

Keep in mind that the ideal settings may vary depending on factors such as your specific camera model, the available light, and your desired outcome.

However, here are some general recommendations to get you started:

1. Shoot in RAW format: RAW files offer more flexibility during post-processing, allowing you to make adjustments without losing image quality.
2. Use manual mode (M): This mode enables you to have complete control over aperture, shutter speed, and ISO settings, which is essential for capturing the dynamic lighting conditions of a sunrise or sunset.
3. Aperture: Choose a mid-range aperture setting, such as f/8 or f/11. This provides a good depth of field, keeping both the foreground and background in focus. If you want a shallower depth of field or if you are shooting in low light conditions, consider using a wider aperture, such as f/2.8 or f/4.
4. Shutter speed: Select a shutter speed that balances the exposure based on your aperture and ISO settings. For handheld shots, make sure your shutter speed is fast enough to avoid camera shake – typically 1/(focal length) seconds or faster. For example, if you're using a 50mm lens, aim for a shutter speed of 1/50 or faster. When using a tripod, you can experiment with slower shutter speeds to capture more light or create motion blur effects, such as smooth water or streaking clouds.

5. ISO: Start with a low ISO, such as 100 or 200, to minimize noise in your image. If you're shooting handheld and need a faster shutter speed, you may need to increase your ISO. However, be aware that higher ISO values can result in more digital noise.

6. White balance: Set your white balance to "Cloudy" or "Shade" to bring out the warm colors of a sunrise or sunset. Alternatively, you can shoot in Auto White Balance (AWB) and adjust the colors during post-processing if you're working with RAW files.

7. Bracket your exposures: To ensure you capture the perfect exposure, consider using exposure bracketing. This involves taking a series of photos at different exposure levels (e.g., one underexposed, one correctly exposed, and one overexposed), which can later be combined in post-processing or used to select the best shot.

Remember that these settings are merely a starting point. The most important aspect of capturing a beautiful sunrise or sunset is to experiment with different settings and compositions, and to learn from your results.

With practice and patience, you'll be able to capture stunning sunrise and sunset images that truly showcase the beauty of nature's daily light show.

2. A city skyline at night

Embracing the Night: A Love Letter to City Skyline Photography

City skylines at night – the intricate dance of light and darkness, creating a breathtaking symphony of visual harmony. As a photography aficionado, I am thrilled to share my passion for capturing the stunning beauty of cityscapes when the sun goes down, and the urban jungle comes to life.

Join me as we embark on a journey through the night, exploring the art of nighttime city skyline photography and inspiring the photographer within you.

First things first, let's talk about location, location, location! Scouting the perfect vantage point is crucial for capturing a jaw-dropping cityscape. Whether you're perched atop a hill, standing on a bridge, or hanging out on a rooftop (with permission, of course), finding that sweet spot will set the stage for your photographic masterpiece.

Just like a well-tailored suit, a great location can elevate your city skyline shot from "nice" to "whoa, that's a framer!"

Stability is the name of the game when it comes to nighttime photography. Unless you have the steady hands of a neurosurgeon, a tripod will be your best friend. Not only will it help eliminate camera shake, but it will also allow you to experiment with long exposures.

Plus, who wouldn't love a three-legged companion to keep them company in the moonlit hours?

Let's dive into the deep end of camera settings. Nighttime cityscapes demand a delicate balance between aperture, shutter speed, and ISO. A wide aperture (low f-number) allows you to capture more light, while a slower shutter speed creates the opportunity for those mesmerizing light trails.

Just don't forget to keep your ISO in check, as we wouldn't want digital noise to crash our nighttime photography party!
Composition is key, and as they say, "variety is the spice of life." You can't go wrong with the tried-and-true rule of thirds, but don't be afraid to experiment with different angles and perspectives.

Get down low, climb up high, or even tilt your camera for a fresh take on the city skyline. After all, fortune favors the bold (and the creative).
Capturing reflections can add an extra layer of magic to your nighttime cityscape.

Seek out bodies of water, glass windows, or even puddles to mirror the dazzling display of lights. Remember, the city skyline is a visual feast, and reflections are the cherry on top.

When it comes to post-processing, subtlety is your ally. Adjusting the contrast, shadows, and highlights can enhance the drama of your nighttime cityscape.

However, much like adding hot sauce to a dish, a little goes a long way. Keep things tasteful, and your city skyline will shine.
Finally, let's address the smartphone conundrum. Fear not, my mobile-wielding friends, for stunning nighttime cityscapes can be captured with the little device in your pocket.

With the right composition, a steady surface, and a touch of editing magic, you too can create a cityscape that will have your social media followers swooning.

Nighttime city skyline photography is a thrilling adventure that allows us to see our urban surroundings in a new light (pun intended). So, grab your camera, venture into the night, and let the dazzling display of city lights inspire your creativity.

After all, as they say, "When the sun goes down, the photographer's playground comes to life." Okay, nobody says that, but maybe they should! Happy shooting!

Camera settings

Capturing the perfect nighttime city skyline requires a combination of the right camera settings and some experimentation. Keep in mind that the ideal settings may vary depending on factors such as your specific camera model, the available light, and your desired outcome.

However, here are some general recommendations to get you started:

1. Shoot in RAW format: RAW files offer more flexibility during post-processing, allowing you to make adjustments without losing image quality.
2. Use manual mode (M) or aperture priority mode (A/Av): These modes allow you to have control over aperture, shutter speed, and ISO settings, which is essential for capturing the dynamic lighting conditions of a nighttime city skyline.
3. Aperture: Choose a mid-range to small aperture setting, such as f/8 or f/16. This provides a good depth of field, keeping both the foreground and background in focus. If you're shooting with a fast lens and want to achieve a shallower depth of field or isolate specific elements, consider using a wider aperture, such as f/2.8 or f/4.
4. Shutter speed: Use a slow shutter speed to capture more light and create a well-exposed image. Typical shutter speeds for nighttime cityscapes range from a few seconds to 30 seconds or longer,

depending on the available light and desired effect. Remember to use a tripod when working with slow shutter speeds to avoid camera shake and ensure sharp images.

5. ISO: Start with a low ISO, such as 100 or 200, to minimize noise in your image. Depending on the available light, you may need to increase your ISO slightly. However, be aware that higher ISO values can result in more digital noise.

6. White balance: Set your white balance to "Tungsten" or "Incandescent" to counteract the warm color cast from artificial city lights. Alternatively, you can shoot in Auto White Balance (AWB) and adjust the colors during post-processing if you're working with RAW files.

7. Use a tripod: A sturdy tripod is essential for achieving sharp images when working with slow shutter speeds. A tripod will also allow you to fine-tune your composition and framing without the risk of camera shake.

8. Use a cable release or self-timer: To avoid introducing camera shake when pressing the shutter button, use a cable release or your camera's built-in self-timer.

The most important aspect of capturing a stunning nighttime city skyline is to experiment with different settings and compositions, and to learn from your results.

3. A local landmark or historical monument

Capturing Timeless Beauty: The Art of Photographing Local Landmarks and Historical Monuments

Photography is the magical art of freezing time, capturing memories, and telling stories through a single frame. As a photography enthusiast, there's no better feeling than immortalizing the beauty of your local landmarks or historical monuments.

By photographing these symbolic structures, you don't just preserve memories; you also capture the essence of the community and its history.

Picture this: a local landmark, standing tall against the backdrop of a vibrant sunset, begging to be captured in its full glory. These iconic structures offer an unparalleled opportunity to flex your creative muscles, experiment with new techniques, and connect with your environment.

So, let's dive into the enchanting world of photographing local landmarks and historical monuments, and unlock the secrets to creating awe-inspiring images. Don't worry; we won't "shutter" at your questions!

Step 1: Get Acquainted with Your Subject

The key to capturing the soul of a landmark lies in knowing its history, purpose, and architectural features. Do some research, learn the stories behind it, and uncover the emotions it evokes. You'll soon find yourself seeing the monument through fresh eyes, and this newfound perspective will undoubtedly shine through your photographs.

Step 2: Timing is Everything

When it comes to photographing landmarks, timing is crucial. The early bird gets the worm, or in this case, the perfect shot! Sunrise and sunset hours, also known as the golden hours, provide the ideal lighting conditions. Not an early riser? No problem, night photography can also yield striking results, showcasing the monument in a different light (pun intended).

Step 3: The Power of Perspective

Perspective is a photographer's secret weapon, capable of transforming an ordinary scene into an extraordinary masterpiece. Don't be afraid to experiment with different angles and viewpoints.

Get down low, climb up high, or take a step back— sometimes, the best shot is right around the corner. Remember, rules are meant to be broken, so feel free to "defocus" on traditional compositions and forge your own path.

Step 4: Embrace the Elements

Don't shy away from adverse weather conditions; instead, use them to your advantage. Rain can create captivating reflections, fog adds an air of mystery, and snow transforms your local landmark into a winter wonderland.

Mother Nature is full of surprises, and sometimes she's the best photo assistant you could ask for!

Step 5: The Human Connection

Including people in your photographs can add depth and emotion to the scene. They can also help convey the scale of a monument, making it even more impressive. Observe the interactions between visitors and the landmark, and wait for the decisive moment to press the shutter button.

Step 6: Editing Magic

In the digital age, post-processing is where the magic happens. Don't be afraid to enhance your images using editing software, but remember to strike a balance between artistic expression and authenticity. A well-edited photo can elevate your work from ordinary to extraordinary, so don't "neglect" the negatives!

Photographing local landmarks and historical monuments is a rewarding and exhilarating endeavor. As you hone your skills, you'll find yourself falling in love with these iconic structures all over again, and you'll be creating a visual narrative that resonates with viewers for years to come.

So, pick up your camera, embrace your inner Ansel Adams, and start capturing the magic!

Camera settings

While the ideal camera settings depend on the specific lighting conditions, subject, and your creative vision, here are some general guidelines to help you capture stunning images of local landmarks and historical monuments:

1. Aperture: Start with an aperture between f/8 and f/16 for a deeper depth of field, ensuring both the foreground and background remain in focus. However, if you want to isolate the subject or create a dreamy, blurred background, opt for a wider aperture (lower f-number).
2. Shutter Speed: To avoid camera shake, choose a shutter speed that's at least the inverse of your focal length (e.g., 1/50s for a 50mm lens). For night photography or capturing motion, you may need a slower shutter speed (e.g., 1-30s). In this case, use a tripod to ensure sharp images.
3. ISO: Keep your ISO as low as possible (e.g., 100-200) to minimize noise and maintain image

quality. In low-light conditions, you may need to increase the ISO (e.g., 800-3200), but be mindful of the noise levels.

4. White Balance: Set your white balance according to the lighting conditions, or use the auto white balance (AWB) setting. For more precise control, shoot in RAW format, allowing you to adjust the white balance during post-processing.

5. Focus: Use manual focus or single-point autofocus to ensure your subject remains sharp. For moving subjects or scenes with lots of activity, consider using continuous autofocus (AF-C) or tracking modes.

6. Drive Mode: Use single-shot mode for most situations, but switch to continuous shooting (burst mode) if you want to capture a series of images in rapid succession.

7. Exposure Compensation: To fine-tune your exposure, use the exposure compensation feature, adjusting it in increments of +1 or -1, depending on whether you want a brighter or darker image.

8. Bracketing: To ensure you capture the perfect exposure, consider using the exposure bracketing feature, which takes multiple shots at different exposure levels.

The best settings may vary depending on your specific situation. Always experiment with different settings to find the perfect combination for your vision, and don't be afraid to think outside the box! Happy shooting!

4. A close-up of a colorful flower

A Symphony of Petals - An Ode to Close-Up Flower Photography

Ladies and gentlemen, prepare to embark on a vibrant journey through the intimate world of close-up flower photography! It is said that beauty lies in the eyes of the beholder, but I dare you to resist the allure of a macro shot of a radiant bloom.

Bursting with color and life, close-up flower photography is a symphony of petals that harmonizes the senses, evokes deep emotions, and, let's face it, makes you want to sniff your screen. (Disclaimer: I do not recommend this activity. I am not responsible for any sneezes, sniffles, or dirty screens.)

A Passionate Palette:

Picture this: a dew-speckled rose, its velvety petals displaying a passionate palette of reds and pinks. Each shade is a passionate love letter to Mother Nature, composing an intoxicating visual sonnet.
A close-up photograph captures the rose's essence, revealing the delicate intricacies of its petals, the grace of its curves, and the tender touch of morning sunlight.

It's the kind of image that makes you want to serenade your computer, crooning "O Rose, thou art sick!"

Dive into the Depths of Detail:

Close-up flower photography is a celebration of the minutiae, a dive into the depths of detail. From the intricate veins of a lily to the whimsical curves of an orchid, close-up shots elevate our appreciation of nature's masterpieces.

The vibrant hues of a tulip suddenly seem otherworldly, and you'll find yourself pondering whether the petals of a sunflower are, in fact, made of pure sunshine. (Spoiler alert: they're not, but isn't it a delightful thought?)

The Hidden World of Pollinators:

Don't forget the importance of our tiny, buzzing friends! Close-up photography often captures the hidden world of pollinators.

From bees frolicking amongst stamens to butterflies perched on petals, these minuscule maestros of the floral world are just as captivating as the flowers themselves. They're the secret sauce that makes the flower burger a delectable treat. (Note: No flowers were harmed in the making of this metaphor.)

The Power of Perspective:

It's all about perspective, my dear friends! Close-up flower photography allows us to view our favorite blooms from an entirely new angle. We're no longer limited to admiring flowers from a distance, like lovestruck teenagers gazing at their crush from afar.

With a macro lens, we can swoop in for the close-up, transforming ourselves into floral detectives, investigating the secrets hidden within each petal, stamen, and pistil. (Elementary, my dear Watson!)

The Joy of Experimentation:

Embrace the spirit of adventure! Experiment with different angles, lighting, and backgrounds to create visual poetry that will leave your audience breathless. Play with selective focus, bokeh, and other creative techniques to elevate your close-up flower shots to the realm of fine art.

And, if the mood strikes you, slap on a wide-angle lens, sit back, and marvel at the sheer absurdity of a daffodil with a fish-eye view. (Trust me, it's a hoot!)

In conclusion, my fellow photography enthusiasts, a close-up of a colorful flower is more than just a snapshot of nature's beauty.

It's an invitation to explore the hidden worlds within each bloom, a chance to witness the intimate dance between light and color, and an opportunity to immortalize the fleeting moments of life's vibrant symphony.

So, grab your camera, head out into the great outdoors, and capture the essence of a flower, one petal at a

Camera settings

When venturing into the realm of close-up flower photography, selecting the right camera settings can make all the difference. Here are some of the best camera settings to help you capture those mesmerizing shots:

1. Aperture: Opt for a medium to small aperture (e.g., f/8 to f/16) to ensure a good depth of field, keeping more of the flower in focus. If you want a dreamy, blurred background (bokeh), you can experiment with a larger aperture (e.g., f/2.8 to f/5.6), but be aware that this will narrow your depth of field.
2. Shutter Speed: Choose a fast shutter speed (e.g., 1/250s or faster) to minimize motion blur from handholding the camera or the flower swaying in the wind. If you're using a tripod and there's minimal movement, you can afford a slower shutter speed.
3. ISO: Keep the ISO low (e.g., 100-400) to minimize noise and achieve the best image quality. In low light conditions or when using a fast shutter speed,

you may need to increase the ISO, but be mindful
of the noise levels.

4. Focus Mode: Select manual focus (MF) or
    autofocus with single-shot mode (AF-S/One-Shot
    AF) for precise control over the focus point. This
    will help you focus on the exact part of the flower
    you want to be sharp.

5. Drive Mode: Utilize single-shot mode to have
    complete control over each frame. However, if
    you're chasing those elusive pollinators, consider
    continuous shooting mode (burst mode) to
    increase your chances of capturing the perfect
    moment.

6. White Balance: Choose the appropriate white
    balance setting (e.g., daylight or cloudy) to
    accurately represent the colors of your subject.
    Alternatively, shoot in RAW format to have the
    flexibility to adjust white balance during post-
    processing.

7. Exposure Compensation: Depending on the
    lighting conditions and the colors of the flower,
    you may need to adjust the exposure compensation
    (+/-) to achieve the desired brightness or mood.

Remember, these settings are a starting point, and the
best results come from experimenting and adapting to the
specific conditions of your shoot. Embrace your inner
creative spirit, and let the petals be your muse!

5. An interesting street scene

The Alluring Dance of Light and Life: A Street Scene Symphony

Imagine a vibrant canvas bursting with colors, a living, breathing masterpiece teeming with stories waiting to be captured. That's the magic of an interesting street scene!

It's a photographer's playground, filled with unique characters, dramatic lighting, and unpredictable moments.

This swirling cocktail of life presents a boundless opportunity for photographers to showcase their artistry while immortalizing the fleeting beauty of the everyday. Picture a bustling market, alive with the hum of commerce, as merchants peddle their wares and customers haggle with gusto.

The kaleidoscope of colors from the fruits and vegetables, the delightful aroma of freshly baked bread, and the cacophony of voices blend together, creating a symphony of sensory delights. And then, like a cherry on top, the sun casts its golden rays, setting the stage for a breathtaking shot. Oh, the light! That fickle, flirtatious mistress that can make or break a photograph. But, when it all comes together, it's like witnessing the birth of a visual poem.

Now, let's dive deeper into the sea of humanity that populates this fascinating street scene. It's said that every face tells a story, and the street photographer's mission is to capture those tales before they vanish into the ether.

Observe the old man with the weathered face, his furrowed brow a testament to a life of labor and wisdom. Or the young couple, their eyes locked in an intimate gaze, as if no one else exists in the world. And let's not forget the mischievous child, caught red-handed with a stolen apple, a cheeky grin that speaks volumes. It's a veritable smorgasbord of emotions and narratives, an endless buffet for the photographer's creative appetite.

The art of street photography is a delicate dance, a balancing act between observation and intrusion. As photographers, we strive to be invisible, blending into the background like chameleons armed with cameras. We tiptoe around the edges of life, hunting for that decisive moment when everything aligns, and the shutter clicks.

There's a certain thrill in being an invisible observer, a stealthy ninja photographer, if you will. In the words of the great Henri Cartier-Bresson, "The most difficult thing for me is a portrait. You have to try and put your camera between the skin of a person and his shirt."

Beyond the human element, the stage itself plays a crucial role in shaping a compelling street scene. The graffiti-adorned walls, the cobblestone streets, the architectural

marvels - each adds texture and character to the urban
tapestry. They're like the spices that bring out the flavors
in a delicious dish, elevating the scene from mundane to
magnificent.

And, speaking of dishes, don't forget the street food
vendors, those culinary magicians who conjure
gastronomic delights from their humble carts. Their
wares, much like the surrounding atmosphere, are a feast
for the senses and a fantastic subject for photography.

An interesting street scene offers a treasure trove of
photographic opportunities, an invitation to explore the
vibrant tapestry of life. So, fellow photographers, I urge
you to grab your trusty camera, hit the streets, and let
your creativity run wild!

After all, the world is your canvas, and every moment is a
brushstroke waiting to be captured. And remember, as
the great photographer Elliott Erwitt once said, "The
whole point of taking pictures is so that you don't have to
explain things with words." Now, go forth and let your
lens do the talking!

Camera Settings

To capture the essence of an interesting street scene,
consider the following camera settings as a starting point.
Keep in mind that every situation is unique, and you may

need to adjust these settings based on specific lighting conditions and desired outcomes.

1. Aperture: Use a wide aperture (f/2.8 to f/5.6) to isolate your subject and create a shallow depth of field. This will help blur the background, drawing attention to your main subject. If you want more of the scene to be in focus, opt for a smaller aperture (f/8 to f/11).
2. Shutter Speed: Choose a faster shutter speed (1/125s to 1/500s) to freeze motion and capture sharp images, especially in dynamic scenes. If you want to convey a sense of motion or blur moving elements, try slower shutter speeds (1/30s to 1/8s), but remember to use a tripod or practice steady hand-holding techniques to avoid camera shake.
3. ISO: Keep the ISO as low as possible (100-400) for minimal noise and optimal image quality. However, in low-light situations or when using faster shutter speeds, you may need to increase the ISO (800-3200) to maintain proper exposure.
4. Focus Mode: Use single-shot autofocus (AF-S or One Shot) for stationary subjects or continuous autofocus (AF-C or AI Servo) for moving subjects to ensure sharp focus.
5. Drive Mode: Set your camera to single-shot mode for precise control over the timing of each shot, or use burst mode (continuous shooting) to capture multiple frames in quick succession, increasing the chances of getting the perfect shot.

6. White Balance: Set your white balance to "Auto" for most situations, allowing your camera to adjust the color temperature based on the lighting conditions. For more control, you can manually set the white balance to match the specific light source (e.g., daylight, shade, tungsten, fluorescent).

7. File Format: Shoot in RAW format to maximize image quality and retain more details for post-processing flexibility. If you prefer minimal post-processing, you can shoot in JPEG format, but keep in mind that this may limit your editing capabilities later on.

To truly master street photography, always be prepared to adapt to the ever-changing conditions of the street.

6. A dramatic weather event (e.g., storm clouds, lightning)

Embracing the Tempest: A Journey into Capturing Dramatic Weather

Imagine this: The sky is a breathtaking canvas of charcoal grays and deep purples, the wind roars like a freight train, and the air crackles with electricity.

No, this isn't the scene from a Hollywood blockbuster or the latest end-of-the-world novel. This is the exhilarating world of dramatic weather photography! Strap on your raincoats, folks, and join me on a whirlwind journey (pun intended) into the art of capturing nature's most mesmerizing displays.

Embracing the Storm

As a photography expert, I am often asked, "Why dramatic weather?" The answer is simple: because it's absolutely thrilling! There's something magical about witnessing the raw power of Mother Nature and immortalizing it in a photograph.

When you're out there in the midst of a storm, it's like being a part of an exclusive, adrenaline-fueled adventure—minus the perils of storm-chasing, of course!

The Palette of the Sky

Storm clouds are the pièce de résistance of any dramatic weather event. It's as if the sky transforms into a moody artist, painting masterpieces with every shade of gray imaginable.

The beauty of storm clouds is that they're ever-changing. One moment they're delicate wisps, the next they're swelling and billowing like a boiling cauldron. With every click of the shutter, you're capturing a unique moment that will never exist again. How's that for exclusivity?

Electrifying Performances

Then there's lightning—nature's very own fireworks display. Few things are as awe-inspiring as the sight of an electric bolt tearing through the sky, illuminating the landscape with a blinding, otherworldly light.

Photographing lightning can be a challenge, but when you nail that perfect shot, you'll feel like Zeus himself, wielding the power of the heavens. Just don't forget to bring a lightning-fast reflex with you (and maybe a sturdy tripod)!

Dancing with the Rain

And who can forget about rain? The way it falls in delicate droplets or pelts the ground with the fury of a thousand tiny drummers. Rain can add an ethereal quality to your images, creating a moody atmosphere that invites the viewer to step into the scene and feel the dampness on their skin. It's like a free special effects package from Mother Nature herself!

Just be sure to protect your gear from the elements (unless you're a fan of expensive paperweights).

The Beauty of the Aftermath

After the storm has passed, don't be too hasty to pack up and head home. The aftermath of a dramatic weather event can be just as stunning as the storm itself. The way the light filters through the dissipating clouds, casting a golden glow on the freshly drenched landscape, is a sight to behold.

Keep your eyes peeled for rainbows, too! They're nature's way of saying, "Sorry for the downpour, here's something pretty to make up for it."

Dramatic weather photography offers a unique blend of excitement, challenge, and beauty that few other genres can match. It's an invitation to step out of your comfort zone and embrace the tempest, to find inspiration in the chaos of nature's most powerful displays.

So the next time you hear thunder rumbling in the distance or see the sky growing dark and moody, grab your camera and seize the opportunity to capture something extraordinary. After all, there's no time like the present—especially when it comes to capturing the perfect storm. Happy shooting, fellow adventurers!

Camera Settings

The ideal camera settings for capturing dramatic weather events will vary depending on the specific conditions and your creative intentions. However, here are some general guidelines to help you get started:

1.   Camera mode: Manual (M) or Aperture Priority (A/Av) mode will give you the most control over your settings and allow you to adapt to the changing light and weather conditions.

2.   Aperture: For landscape shots with a deep depth of field, use a smaller aperture (higher f-number), such as f/8 to f/16. For isolating subjects against a moody sky, use a larger aperture (lower f-number), like f/2.8 to f/5.6.

3.   Shutter speed: To freeze raindrops or capture lightning, use a fast shutter speed (1/250s or faster). For creating motion blur in clouds or rain, opt for a slower shutter speed (1/30s to several seconds). For lightning, you may also consider using a longer exposure (e.g., 10-30 seconds) in a dark environment and a tripod to keep the camera stable.

4.   ISO: To minimize noise, start with a low ISO (100-200). Increase the ISO if necessary to achieve the desired shutter speed and aperture combination, but be aware

that higher ISO values will introduce more noise into your image.

5.   White balance: Set your white balance to Auto or Cloudy to accurately capture the colors and mood of the stormy sky.

6.   Focus: Use manual focus or single-point autofocus to ensure that your subject is sharp. For landscapes, focus on a point about one-third into the scene to maximize depth of field.

7.   Image stabilization: If your camera or lens has image stabilization, turn it on to help minimize camera shake, especially when shooting handheld in low light conditions.

8.   File format: Shoot in RAW format to capture the maximum amount of detail and have greater flexibility during post-processing.

9.   Bracketing: In challenging lighting conditions, consider using exposure bracketing to capture a range of exposures that you can later merge into an HDR image.

7. A stunning natural landscape

The Majestic Symphony of Nature: A Journey Through a Stunning Landscape

Oh, the splendor and awe that Mother Nature offers us through her breathtaking landscapes! Every corner of our beautiful planet has an enchanting story to tell, a visual feast for the soul.

Now we'll embark on an adventure through a mesmerizing natural landscape, a symphony of colors and textures that will leave you yearning to grab your camera and capture the wonders of the world.

So, buckle up, as we explore the magnificent orchestra of the natural world, with each element playing its harmonious part in creating a true masterpiece.

The Setting: Picture this: a vast expanse of rolling hills, blanketed by lush, verdant grass, with a backdrop of towering, majestic mountains that pierce the skies. Imagine the gentle embrace of the cool breeze, as it whispers secrets to the swaying trees, and the soft babbling of a crystal-clear river, winding its way through the valley like a shimmering silver ribbon.

This idyllic scene is not only a feast for the eyes but a symphony for the senses – a place where time stands still and the soul rejoices in nature's grandeur.

The Palette of Colors: The sun rises, casting its golden rays upon the landscape, transforming it into a canvas of vibrant colors, as if Mother Nature herself had taken up her paintbrush.

The hills are awash in a warm, golden hue, while the distant mountains are tinged with soft purples and blues, bathed in the first light of day. Flashes of scarlet and orange dance amidst the greenery, as wildflowers bloom, their delicate petals unfurling to greet the morning sun.

This riot of colors weaves a tapestry of natural beauty that would make even Monet envious.
The Symphony of Textures: Our stunning landscape is not only a visual delight but also an intricate symphony of textures, begging to be explored through the lens of a camera. The velvety softness of moss-covered boulders contrasts with the rugged, craggy surfaces of the mountains, while the smooth, glass-like surface of the river reflects the kaleidoscope of colors above.

As the wind rustles through the leaves and tall grasses, it creates a dynamic dance of light and shadow, a visual melody that echoes the harmonious rhythm of nature.

The Captivating Details: In this picturesque scene, it's not just the grand vistas that capture our hearts, but also the myriad of captivating details that await discovery.

The iridescent wings of a dragonfly as it hovers above the water, the intricate patterns on the bark of an ancient tree, or the dewdrops that glisten like tiny jewels on the petals of a flower – each of these minute wonders is a testament to the incredible beauty and complexity of the natural world.

The Enchantment of Light: As the day progresses, the landscape continues to evolve, with the enchanting play of light transforming the scene before our eyes.
The warm, golden glow of the setting sun casts long shadows, adding depth and drama to the tableau, while the fiery hues of twilight paint the sky in a breathtaking display of color.

As the stars begin to twinkle above, the landscape is bathed in the soft, ethereal light of the moon, casting an air of magic and mystery over the tranquil scene.

In our journey through this stunning natural landscape, we have witnessed the incredible beauty and harmony of the natural world, a symphony of colors, textures, and light that inspires and moves us.

As photographers, we have the privilege of capturing these fleeting moments of wonder, preserving the enchantment of nature for generations to come. So, go forth and explore the hidden gems that our beautiful

Camera Settings

To capture the full essence of the stunning natural landscape described above, it's essential to adjust your camera settings to suit the varying conditions and subjects.

Here are some recommended settings to help you achieve the best results:

1. **Sunrise/Sunset:**
   - Mode: Aperture Priority (Av or A)
   - Aperture: f/8 to f/16 (for a greater depth of field)
   - ISO: 100-200 (to minimize noise)
   - Shutter Speed: Let the camera decide (based on Aperture and ISO)
   - White Balance: Auto or Cloudy/Sunset (to enhance warm tones)
   - Focus: Manual or Single-point Autofocus (to ensure a sharp focus on the desired subject)

2. **Landscapes:**
   - Mode: Aperture Priority (Av or A)
   - Aperture: f/8 to f/16 (for a greater depth of field)
   - ISO: 100 (to minimize noise)
   - Shutter Speed: Let the camera decide (based on Aperture and ISO)
   - White Balance: Auto or Daylight

- Focus: Manual or Single-point Autofocus (to ensure a sharp focus on the desired subject)

3. **Macro Details (flowers, insects, etc.):**
- Mode: Aperture Priority (Av or A) or Manual (M)
- Aperture: f/2.8 to f/8 (for a shallow depth of field and blurred background)
- ISO: 200-800 (depending on lighting conditions)
- Shutter Speed: 1/125s or faster (to freeze motion)
- White Balance: Auto
- Focus: Manual or Macro Autofocus (to achieve a sharp focus on small subjects)

4. **Rivers and Water Reflections:**
- Mode: Aperture Priority (Av or A) or Manual (M)
- Aperture: f/11 to f/16 (for a greater depth of field)
- ISO: 100 (to minimize noise)
- Shutter Speed: 1/30s or slower (to capture smooth water movement)
- White Balance: Auto or Daylight
- Focus: Manual or Single-point Autofocus (to ensure a sharp focus on the desired subject)

5. **Night Photography (stars, moonlit scenes):**
- Mode: Manual (M)
- Aperture: f/2.8 to f/4 (to allow maximum light)
- ISO: 800-3200 (depending on the desired level of noise and brightness)
- Shutter Speed: 15-30 seconds (to capture stars without significant trails)

- White Balance: Auto or Tungsten (to counteract the orange hue of artificial light)
- Focus: Manual (set to infinity for stars)

Don't be afraid to experiment and fine-tune your settings to capture the true magic of the landscape.

8. A group of friends or family members

Family Focused: Capturing the Heart of Togetherness Through Photography

There is an old saying, "A picture is worth a thousand words," and it couldn't be more true when it comes to capturing the priceless moments shared by families and friends.

So, grab your camera and let's dive into the enchanting world of family and friendship photography – where the smiles are plentiful, the laughter is contagious, and the bonds are unbreakable.

The Power of Candid Moments

Family gatherings, weekend barbecues, or a simple evening walk can turn into lifelong memories when you have your camera ready to capture the candid moments that matter.

Candid photography is all about seizing the unscripted, authentic interactions between people, like a spontaneous burst of laughter, a tender hug, or a shared glance between friends. It's these genuine moments, frozen in time, that tell a powerful story of love, connection, and togetherness.

Tip: Always have your camera within reach and be prepared to snap a quick shot. Just remember, when it comes to candid photography, practice makes perfect, so keep clicking!

Group Dynamics: Pose, Snap, Repeat!

When photographing groups of family members or friends, it's important to consider the dynamics of the relationships you're capturing. From the playful banter between siblings to the quiet understanding between lifelong friends, each connection is unique and should be showcased in your images.

A well-composed group photo can be a work of art, highlighting individual personalities while also emphasizing the collective spirit. Experiment with different poses, arrangements, and angles to create a visually appealing and emotionally resonant image.

Tip: Don't be afraid to get creative with your group photos – after all, you're capturing a bunch of fun-loving people, not statues!

The Art of Storytelling

One of the most satisfying aspects of photography is the ability to tell a story through a series of images. By capturing the small moments and subtle details that make up a family or friend gathering, you can create a visual narrative that highlights the unique character of the relationships you're documenting.

To tell a compelling story, look for the little moments that others might overlook – the mischievous grin of a child, the loving gaze of a grandparent, or the shared laughter of old friends.
These are the magical moments that make your photographs come alive and evoke the emotions of the day.

Tip: Remember, the best stories are not always told through the grand gestures, but through the intimate, unguarded moments that reveal the heart and soul of your subjects.

Embrace the Imperfections

In the pursuit of the perfect photo, it's easy to forget that it's the imperfections that make life interesting and unique.
Embrace the outtakes, the funny faces, and the awkward poses – these are the images that remind us that life is beautifully messy and that our loved ones are perfectly imperfect.

Tip: Don't be too hard on yourself if every shot isn't a masterpiece. Some of the most cherished family photographs are the ones that capture the genuine laughter, surprise, and delight of a moment gone awry.

Photographing family and friends is a heartwarming and fulfilling journey that allows us to capture the beauty of human connection and create lasting memories.

Whether it's through candid moments, group dynamics, storytelling, or embracing imperfections, remember that the true magic of photography lies in the love, laughter, and togetherness that binds us all.

So, grab your camera, gather your loved ones, and get ready to create a visual legacy that

Camera Settings

Choosing the right camera settings is crucial to capturing stunning photographs of family and friends. While there's no one-size-fits-all solution, the following recommendations will help you get started:

1. Aperture: For group shots, it's essential to have enough depth of field to ensure that everyone is in focus. Set your aperture to a value between f/5.6 and f/11. For individual or candid shots, you can experiment with a wider aperture (e.g., f/2.8) to create a shallow depth of field and draw attention to your subject.
2. Shutter Speed: To freeze the action and avoid motion blur, use a fast shutter speed. A good starting point is 1/250s. However, you may need to adjust it depending on the lighting conditions and the amount of movement in the scene. If you're shooting in low light, you may need to use a slower shutter speed and a tripod to prevent camera shake.

3. ISO: Keep your ISO as low as possible (e.g., ISO 100 or 200) to minimize noise in your images. However, if you're shooting in low-light conditions or need a faster shutter speed, you may need to increase your ISO. Be aware that raising the ISO can introduce noise and grain to your images, so balance it carefully with the other settings.

4. White Balance: To ensure accurate colors, set your white balance according to the lighting conditions. Most cameras have preset options for daylight, shade, cloudy, tungsten, and fluorescent lighting. Alternatively, you can use the custom white balance setting for even more precise control.

5. Focus Mode: Use continuous autofocus (AI Servo for Canon, AF-C for Nikon) for tracking moving subjects or when capturing candid moments. Switch to single autofocus (One-Shot for Canon, AF-S for Nikon) when taking group shots or posed portraits.

6. Drive Mode: For candid photography, consider using the continuous shooting mode (also known as burst mode) to capture multiple images in rapid succession.

7. Metering Mode: Evaluative or matrix metering generally works well for group photos and candid moments, as it takes into account the entire frame to determine the correct exposure.

The key is to practice and experiment to find the perfect combination that works for you and your subjects.

9. A candid moment between people

The Magic of Candid Moments: Capturing the Essence of Human Connection

Candid moments! Those beautiful, unscripted instances that offer a genuine glimpse into the human experience.

As photographers, we live for these snapshots in time, where genuine emotion and connection between people shine through, unfettered by self-consciousness.

So, buckle up, my fellow shutterbugs, as we delve into the world of candid photography and uncover the secrets to capturing these magical moments.

Now, you might ask, "What makes candid photography so special?" Well, imagine a world where every photograph was posed, every smile carefully curated, and every interaction staged. Sounds pretty dull, doesn't it?

Candid moments, on the other hand, offer a refreshing, unfiltered look at life, capturing the essence of human connection in its rawest form. It's like a peek behind the curtain, revealing the beauty, humor, and vulnerability that lies within us all.

So, how do we immortalize these fleeting moments? Fear not, for I have some tips and tricks up my sleeve that will have you snapping candid masterpieces in no time!

1. Blend into the background: Stealth is the name of the game here, folks. The less noticeable you are, the more likely your subjects will act naturally, unaware of your camera's gaze. Channel your inner ninja, dress in inconspicuous attire, and stay on your toes – you never know when the perfect moment will present itself!

2. Go telephoto: While it may be tempting to get up close and personal, using a telephoto lens allows you to maintain a comfortable distance from your subjects, avoiding any potential awkwardness. Plus, it's a great excuse to invest in some shiny new gear (as if we needed one)!

3. Patience is a virtue: Candid moments can't be forced, so it's crucial to bide your time and wait for the magic to unfold before your eyes. Remember, the universe rewards the patient photographer with the most captivating shots. So, find a cozy spot, sit back, and let the world reveal itself to you.

4. Embrace spontaneity: While it's great to have a plan, sometimes the most enchanting moments occur when we least expect them. So, keep your camera at the ready, and don't be afraid to take a detour down that intriguing alley or strike up a conversation with a friendly stranger. Adventure awaits!

5. Tell a story: Candid moments are so much more than pretty pictures – they're a window into the human experience. So, when composing your shot, consider the emotions and relationships at play, and strive to tell a compelling story through your lens. After all, a picture is worth a thousand words, right?

6. Practice makes perfect: Like any skill, mastering candid photography takes time and dedication. So, don't be discouraged if your early attempts don't quite hit the mark. Keep honing your craft, learning from your mistakes, and before you know it, you'll be capturing the essence of human connection like a pro.

The magic of candid moments lies in their authenticity, revealing the beauty, humor, and vulnerability of the human experience. By mastering the art of blending into the background, exercising patience, and embracing spontaneity, you'll be well on your way to capturing these fleeting moments for posterity.

So, grab your camera, channel your inner ninja, and venture forth to document the wonder of life unfolding before your eyes. Good luck, and may the candid moments be ever in your favor!

Camera Settings

To capture candid moments effectively, it's essential to consider the right camera settings. Here's a rundown of the best settings to help you achieve those stunning candid shots:

1. Aperture: Opt for a wide aperture (low f-number) to create a shallow depth of field. This isolates your subjects from the background, drawing the viewer's attention to the moment you've captured. Commonly used apertures for this purpose range from f/1.8 to f/4.

2. Shutter Speed: Use a fast shutter speed to freeze motion and avoid blur, especially when capturing spontaneous interactions. A good starting point is 1/250th of a second, but you may need to go faster (1/500 or 1/1000) if your subjects are moving quickly.

3. ISO: Set your ISO according to the available light. In bright conditions, a low ISO (100-200) is ideal, while in low-light situations, you may need to increase the ISO (800-1600) to maintain a fast shutter speed. However, be cautious of pushing the ISO too high, as this can introduce noise into your images.

4. Focus Mode: Choose continuous or servo autofocus (AI Servo for Canon, AF-C for Nikon, and similar modes for other brands) to track moving subjects and ensure they remain in focus. This mode is particularly useful when capturing candid moments involving movement.

5. Drive Mode: Select continuous or burst shooting mode to take multiple shots in quick succession. This increases

your chances of capturing that perfect candid moment as it unfolds.

6. Metering Mode: Opt for matrix or evaluative metering (depending on your camera brand) to ensure even exposure across the entire frame. This is particularly helpful when dealing with unpredictable lighting conditions or rapidly changing scenes.

7. White Balance: Use auto white balance (AWB) for most situations, as it typically does a decent job of accurately reproducing colors. However, if you find the colors to be off, you can always adjust the white balance in post-processing.

8. Image Stabilization: If your lens or camera offers image stabilization (IS or VR), it's a good idea to turn it on. This can help minimize the effects of camera shake and result in sharper images, especially when shooting handheld.

10. A unique architectural detail

The Art of Capturing Architectural Wonders: Zooming in on Unique Details

Imagine standing before an awe-inspiring building, a true architectural marvel that stirs the soul and begs to be immortalized in a photograph. The intricate details, the soaring spires, the delicate curves, and the bold lines - all conspiring to make this piece of architecture a photographer's dream.

Before we begin our visual journey, let's pack our camera bags with essentials. A keen eye for detail, a dash of creativity, and a hearty dose of enthusiasm - these are the ingredients that will transform your architectural photography into a stunning work of art.
Don't forget your camera, lenses, and tripod - after all, even the most eagle-eyed of photographers need their trusty gear!

As we embark on our quest for capturing architectural details, the first stop is 'Perspective Plaza.' A fresh perspective can make all the difference in the world, and sometimes that means getting up close and personal with your subject.
So, put on your most comfortable shoes, and don't be afraid to step back, lean in, or even lie down to discover the most breathtaking angle. Remember, there's no one-size-

fits-all approach when it comes to perspective - creativity is your compass!

Next on our itinerary is 'Lighting Lane,' a dazzling destination where shadows and highlights dance in perfect harmony. Just as an artist paints with colors, a photographer paints with light. As the sun rises and sets, it casts a unique glow upon the architectural details, so timing is everything.

Chase that golden hour, brave the blue hour, and embrace the moody clouds - the perfect lighting could be just a moment away. And if natural light is playing hard to get, never fear; artificial lighting is here! Experiment with external flashes or even a simple torch to highlight those exquisite details.

Now, we venture into the bustling metropolis of 'Composition City.' Here, the rule of thirds is the law of the land, and leading lines guide the viewer's eye through the urban jungle.

When framing your shot, consider the relationship between the architectural detail and its surroundings.
Can you create a striking juxtaposition, or perhaps a harmony of patterns? The secret to a well-composed photograph is finding balance - much like a tightrope walker or a yoga master, but with less sweat and more pixels.

But wait! Our journey would be incomplete without a visit to the whimsical world of 'Post-Processing Park.' Here, digital wizards wield their mighty Photoshop wands, transforming raw images into vibrant visual stories.

Adjusting the contrast, saturation, and sharpness can breathe new life into your photograph, emphasizing the unique architectural details you've captured. But beware, young Padawan; with great power comes great responsibility. Tread lightly on the sliders and resist the dark side of over-editing!

And there you have it, my fellow photography enthusiasts: a whirlwind tour through the enchanting realm of photographing unique architectural details.

Remember, your camera is your magic wand, and the world is your canvas. Embrace your inner artist, and let your imagination soar as high as those architectural marvels you're capturing. Now, go forth and create your photographic symphony - one stunning detail at a time!

Camera Settings

While the best camera settings for capturing unique architectural details can vary depending on the specific conditions and desired outcome, here's a general guideline to get you started:

1. Aperture: Aim for an aperture setting between f/8 and f/16. This range generally provides a greater depth of field, ensuring that both the architectural detail and the surrounding context remain in focus. However, if you want to isolate the detail and create a pleasing background blur, consider using a wider aperture like f/2.8 or f/4.

2. Shutter Speed: Choose a shutter speed that balances the available light and your desired depth of field. In bright conditions, a faster shutter speed (such as 1/250 or 1/500) will help to prevent overexposure. In low-light situations, you may need to use a slower shutter speed (such as 1/30 or 1/60) and a tripod to prevent camera shake and ensure sharpness.

3. ISO: Keep your ISO as low as possible (100 or 200) to minimize noise and preserve image quality. If you're shooting in low-light conditions and don't have a tripod, you may need to increase your ISO to maintain a suitable shutter speed. However, be aware that increasing ISO can introduce noise to your image, so it's a delicate balance.

4. White Balance: Set your white balance to "Auto" or select a specific setting based on the prevailing lighting conditions (e.g., "Daylight" for outdoor shots or "Tungsten" for indoor shots with incandescent lighting). Adjusting the white balance helps to ensure accurate color representation in your architectural photographs.

5. Focus Mode: Use "Single Shot Autofocus" (AF-S) or "Manual Focus" (MF) to precisely focus on the architectural detail you want to capture. If the detail

is part of a larger, moving scene, you may want to consider "Continuous Autofocus" (AF-C) to track the subject as it moves.

6. Drive Mode: Select "Single Shot" if you're capturing a stationary subject, or "Continuous" if you're shooting multiple frames of a moving scene. The latter can be useful for creating HDR images, where multiple exposures are combined to achieve greater dynamic range.

7. File Format: Shoot in RAW format if possible, as this provides the most flexibility in post-processing. RAW files contain more image data and allow you to make adjustments to exposure, white balance, and other settings without significant quality loss.

11. Street art or graffiti

Capturing the Colorful Canvases of the Streets - The Art of Photographing Graffiti

Graffiti and street art are beautiful, spontaneous expressions of creativity that can be found in almost every corner of the urban jungle. With an abundance of vibrant colors and eye-catching designs, these urban masterpieces provide a fantastic subject for photography enthusiasts who want to capture the essence of a city's soul.

So, if you're ready to embark on a thrilling and colorful journey, let's dive into the world of graffiti photography, one spray-painted wall at a time!

1. **Embrace the Urban Environment**
The first step in your graffiti photography adventure is to become one with the city. Wander the streets, explore alleyways, and venture into abandoned buildings. Look for hidden gems that are waiting to be discovered and immortalized through your lens. Remember, sometimes the best masterpieces are found off the beaten path. And who knows, you might just stumble upon the next Banksy!

2. **Get the Right Gear**
While your smartphone might be sufficient for capturing the occasional snap, a proper camera can make all the difference when it comes to graffiti photography. Choose a

versatile camera with a good-quality wide-angle lens to ensure you can capture the entire artwork, especially in tight spaces. A tripod is also essential for low-light situations or when you want to get creative with long exposures. And don't forget a comfortable pair of walking shoes – your feet will thank you later!

3. Play with Perspectives

Graffiti art is often found in unconventional locations, so don't be afraid to get creative with your angles and perspectives. Experiment with different viewpoints, such as shooting from below to accentuate the towering height of the artwork or from above to capture the surrounding context. Incorporating interesting elements in the foreground or background can also add depth and dimension to your photos. After all, it's not just about the art, it's about telling the story of its place in the urban landscape.

4. Timing is Everything

As the saying goes, timing is everything – especially in photography. To make your graffiti photos stand out from the crowd, try shooting during the golden hour, when the warm and diffused light can give your images a magical glow. Alternatively, take advantage of the unique shadows and contrasts created during the day or experiment with the artificial lights of the city at night. You might just find that the perfect shot is waiting for you at the most unexpected time!

5. **Respect the Art and the Artist**

Graffiti and street art are often ephemeral, with pieces being painted over or removed, so it's important to respect and preserve their fleeting nature. Always credit the artist when possible, and never alter the artwork without permission. It's also crucial to be aware of your surroundings, as some locations might be private property or have safety risks. Remember, the goal is to capture and celebrate these urban masterpieces, not to cause harm or create unnecessary conflict.

6. **Share Your Passion**

Once you've captured the perfect shot, don't keep it all to yourself! Share your passion for graffiti photography by posting your images on social media, participating in photography forums, or submitting your work to galleries and exhibitions. By sharing your art, you'll not only inspire others to explore the captivating world of street art, but you'll also help to promote the talented artists who create these incredible urban canvases.

Photographing graffiti and street art is an exciting and rewarding way to immerse yourself in the vibrant culture of a city. By following these tips and keeping an open mind, you'll soon be capturing breathtaking images that tell the stories of these colorful urban masterpieces.

So, grab your camera, lace up your walking shoes, and unleash your inner shutterbug – the streets await!

Camera Settings

Now list the best camera settings for the above.

When photographing graffiti and street art, there is no one-size-fits-all solution for camera settings, as different situations and lighting conditions will require adjustments. However, here are some general guidelines to help you get started:

1. Aperture: Use a smaller aperture (higher f-number) like f/8 or f/11 to achieve a deeper depth of field, ensuring that both the graffiti and the surrounding environment are in focus. In low-light conditions, you may need to use a wider aperture (lower f-number) like f/2.8 or f/4 to allow more light into the camera.

2. Shutter Speed: Start with a shutter speed of around 1/125s to 1/250s to freeze motion and avoid camera shake. If you're using a tripod or experimenting with long exposures, you can use slower shutter speeds like 1s or even 30s, depending on the desired effect.

3. ISO: Keep the ISO as low as possible (e.g., ISO 100 or 200) to minimize noise and ensure the best image quality. In low-light conditions or when shooting handheld without a tripod, you may need to increase the ISO to 800 or even 1600 to maintain a fast enough shutter speed.

4. White Balance: Set the white balance according to the available light. For natural daylight, use the 'Daylight' or 'Sunny' setting. For overcast skies or

shade, try the 'Cloudy' setting. When shooting at night or under artificial light, experiment with the 'Tungsten' or 'Fluorescent' settings to achieve accurate color representation.

5. Focus Mode: Use autofocus (AF) with a single focus point to ensure sharp focus on the graffiti or street art. If you're photographing a scene with a lot of depth, consider switching to manual focus (MF) to fine-tune the focus point.

6. Drive Mode: Set your camera to single-shot mode for most situations. If you're trying to capture the perfect moment, such as an artist at work or a dynamic scene, switch to continuous shooting mode to increase your chances of getting the perfect shot.

7. Image Format: Shoot in RAW format, if available, to have more flexibility and control over post-processing. If your camera doesn't support RAW or you prefer a smaller file size, use the highest quality JPEG setting.

12. A pet or interesting animal

Lights, Camera, Paws! Unleashing the Joy of Animal Photography

Have you ever wished you could capture the true essence of your furry, feathery, or scaly companion? Well, it's time to unleash your inner photographer and embark on a thrilling adventure of animal photography!

Not only will you create cherished memories, but you'll also discover the boundless joy that comes from combining your love for animals and photography. So, strap on your camera, grab a treat or two, and let's venture into the wild world of pet and animal photography!

A Tail of Two Techniques

To begin your journey, let's explore the two main techniques in animal photography: candid and posed. Candid shots are the unscripted, spontaneous moments that happen when your pet is just being themselves.

These raw, genuine images often capture the soul of your pet, making them priceless. Posed shots, on the other hand, require a little more planning and patience, but can create beautiful, artistic images that showcase your pet's unique personality.

Whiskers in the Wind: Capturing Candid Shots

Capturing those fleeting candid moments can be a game of cat and mouse, but fear not! Here are some tips to help you snap the purr-fect candid shot:

1. Be Prepared: Have your camera ready at all times! Pets are unpredictable, and you never know when a great moment will present itself.
2. Observe: Study your pet's behavior and anticipate their actions. Knowing when Fluffy loves to chase her tail or when Rex gets a case of the zoomies will help you be in the right place at the right time.
3. Go Low: Get down to your pet's eye level. This perspective not only adds depth to your images but also helps you better connect with your subject.
4. Be Patient: Animal photography is a waiting game. Embrace it and enjoy the process – you might just catch that elusive "unicorn" shot!

Strike a Paws: Mastering the Art of Posed Photography

If you're looking for a more polished image, try your hand at posed photography. Here are some tips to help you guide your pet into the spotlight:

1. Location, Location, Location: Choose a spot that complements your pet's features and personality, whether it's a sun-drenched windowsill or a lush green park.

2. Treats & Toys: Entice your pet with their favorite treats or toys to get their attention and hold it long enough for the perfect shot.

3. Get Creative: Play with props, outfits, or backdrops to bring out the best in your pet. Just remember, comfort is key – if Whiskers looks miserable in that tiny sombrero, it might be time to ditch the props.

4. Lighting Matters: Natural light is your best friend. Find a well-lit area or use the golden hour (the hour after sunrise or before sunset) for that warm, magical glow.

A Snappy Ending

Whether you're chasing butterflies with your camera-wielding cat or directing your dapper dog in a photoshoot, the joy of pet and animal photography is in the journey. It's about bonding with your pet, honing your skills, and creating memories that will last a lifetime.

So, go ahead and let the fur fly – there's a world of whiskers, paws, and feathers waiting to be captured through your lens!

Camera Settings

The "best" camera settings for pet and animal photography can vary depending on the situation and desired outcome. However, here are some general guidelines to help you get started:

1. Shooting Mode: Use Aperture Priority (Av or A) or Shutter Priority (Tv or S) mode. Aperture Priority allows you to control the depth of field, while Shutter Priority lets you control the motion in your images.

2. Aperture: For a shallow depth of field and blurred backgrounds, use a wide aperture (low f-number, such as f/2.8 or f/4). To keep more of the scene in focus, choose a narrower aperture (higher f-number, like f/8 or f/11).

3. Shutter Speed: To freeze motion, use a fast shutter speed (1/500 or faster). For more creative shots with intentional motion blur, experiment with slower shutter speeds (1/30 or slower).

4. ISO: Keep your ISO as low as possible (100 or 200) to minimize noise in your images. Increase it only when necessary, like in low-light situations or when using faster shutter speeds.

5. Focus Mode: Use continuous autofocus (AI Servo or AF-C) to track your pet's movement and keep them in focus as they move around the frame.

6. Drive Mode: Switch to continuous shooting (burst mode) to capture multiple frames per second, increasing your chances of getting the perfect shot.

7. Metering Mode: Use Evaluative/Matrix metering for most situations, as it considers the entire frame when determining the exposure. For high-contrast scenes, consider using Spot or Center-weighted metering.

8. White Balance: Set your white balance according to the lighting conditions, or use Auto White Balance (AWB) if you prefer to adjust it later during post-processing.

Feel free to experiment and adjust them based on your personal style, your pet's behavior, and the specific conditions in which you're shooting.

The key to great animal photography is patience, practice, and a willingness to learn from your experiences. So, go ahead and explore the wonderful world of pet and animal photography with your camera in hand!

13. A long-exposure image of traffic

Lights, Camera, Zoom! Capturing the Dance of Traffic in Long-Exposure Photography

Picture this: a bustling city street at night, cars whizzing by like shooting stars, their headlights painting streaks of light across the canvas of the urban landscape. Sounds like a scene from a sci-fi movie, right?

Well, grab your camera and tripod, because today we're going to explore the art of long-exposure photography, focusing on capturing the mesmerizing dance of traffic!

Before we dive into the heart of the matter, let's get acquainted with the basics. Long-exposure photography, also known as time-exposure or slow-shutter photography, is all about leaving the camera's shutter open for an extended period.

This technique allows you to capture the motion of light and other elements in a way that our eyes simply can't perceive. It's like being handed the keys to a secret world of visual delights!

So, how do you capture the perfect long-exposure image of traffic? Here's a roadmap to get you started:

1. Gear Up: To embark on this thrilling adventure, you'll need a camera with manual controls (preferably a DSLR or mirrorless), a sturdy tripod to keep things steady (nobody likes a shaky masterpiece), and a remote shutter release to avoid camera shake.

2. Location, Location, Location: Scout for the perfect spot with a good vantage point of traffic flow. Bridges and overpasses are prime real estate for this purpose, offering a bird's-eye view of the hypnotic stream of vehicles below. Remember, the busier the street, the more dazzling your photo will be!

3. Timing is Everything: While you can certainly experiment with long-exposure photography during the day, nighttime shots with illuminated car lights create a surreal, otherworldly effect. Blue hour, that magical window of time just after sunset and before full darkness, provides a beautiful backdrop for your light trails.

4. Set Your Camera: With your tripod standing tall and your camera secured, it's time to dial in the settings. Set your camera to manual mode and start with a low ISO (100-200) to minimize noise. Choose a small aperture (f/8 to f/16) for a greater depth of field, and finally, select a shutter speed of 10-30 seconds to capture those glorious light trails. Don't be afraid to experiment with different settings – after all, practice makes perfect!

5. Frame Your Shot: Compose your image by considering the rule of thirds, leading lines, and other photography principles. Visualize the final result, imagining how the light trails will flow through the frame. Remember, a strong composition is worth a thousand likes!

6. Click and Revel: Press the remote shutter release and watch as your camera works its magic. As the shutter remains open, the sensor will gather the light emitted by the moving vehicles, creating those signature streaks we all love. When the exposure is complete, take a peek at your masterpiece – but don't be too hard on yourself if it isn't perfect right away. Adjust your settings, experiment with composition, and keep clicking until you've captured the shot that leaves you breathless.

Long-exposure photography is an incredible way to explore the world around us, and the urban symphony of traffic provides an ideal subject for creating stunning images.

So gear up, set your sights on the nearest bustling street, and get ready to freeze time in a way that even Doc Brown from "Back to the Future" would envy. May the light trails be ever in your favor!

Camera Settings

To capture a long-exposure image of traffic, consider these recommended camera settings as a starting point:

1. Camera Mode: Manual mode (M), allowing you complete control over your settings.
2. ISO: Set a low ISO, typically between 100 and 200, to minimize noise in your image.
3. Aperture: Choose a small aperture, ranging from f/8 to f/16, to ensure a greater depth of field and keep more of the scene in focus.
4. Shutter Speed: Start with a shutter speed of 10-30 seconds, depending on the speed of the traffic and the desired length of the light trails. Feel free to experiment with different durations to find the best result.
5. White Balance: Use the Auto White Balance (AWB) or choose a specific setting, such as Tungsten or Fluorescent, to accommodate the prevailing lighting conditions.
6. Focus: Switch to manual focus, and use the Live View feature or a distant streetlight to set the focus at the desired distance. This will ensure that your camera doesn't struggle to find focus in low-light conditions.
7. Image Format: Shoot in RAW format to preserve the maximum amount of image data, giving you greater flexibility during post-processing.

14. A macro shot of an insect or small creature

The Art of Capturing the Little Wonders: Macro Photography of Insects and Small Creatures

The Miniature Majesty of the Macro World

Have you ever been mesmerized by the intricate beauty of a butterfly's wings or the delicate structure of a spider's web? If so, you're in for a real treat!

These tiny wonders often go unnoticed in our fast-paced lives, but with a little bit of patience and the right techniques, you can capture their remarkable details and bring their miniature majesty to life.

Step 1: Gear Up for the Macro Adventure

Before you embark on your macro photography journey, you'll need to equip yourself with the right tools. A dedicated macro lens, such as a 100mm f/2.8, is a fantastic choice, offering a 1:1 magnification ratio and a razor-sharp focus on your tiny subjects. However, if you're on a budget, extension tubes or a reverse lens adapter can be a cost-effective alternative.

A sturdy tripod is your best friend in macro photography, as it provides stability and minimizes camera shake, ensuring that your tiny subjects stay sharp and in focus.

Additionally, consider investing in a remote shutter release or using your camera's self-timer to further reduce camera movement.

Step 2: Embrace the Hunt for Tiny Treasures

Finding the perfect insect or small creature to photograph can be an adventure in itself. Wander through gardens, forests, or even your own backyard, keeping your eyes peeled for hidden gems. Patience is key, and remember: "the early bird catches the worm" – or, in this case, the stunning dew-covered spiderweb.

Step 3: Master the Art of Composition and Lighting

When it comes to macro photography, composition is crucial. Experiment with different angles and perspectives to find the most visually striking shot. Don't be afraid to get up close and personal with your subject – after all, that's what macro photography is all about! As they say, "if you're not getting dirty, you're not doing it right."

Natural light is your best ally, but don't shy away from using an external flash or a reflector to enhance your subject's details and add depth to your images. The magic hour – the time just after sunrise or before sunset – often provides the most enchanting light for macro photography.

Step 4: Master the Art of Focus

Achieving tack-sharp focus in macro photography can be a challenge, as the depth of field is often shallow. Manual focus is typically the way to go, allowing you to fine-tune the focus on your subject's most interesting features, such as the eyes of an insect or the hairs of a caterpillar. And remember: practice makes perfect!

Step 5: Post-Processing and Beyond

Once you've captured your macro masterpiece, it's time for some post-processing magic. Software like Adobe Lightroom or Photoshop can help you fine-tune your image, enhance colors, and bring out the tiniest details. But remember, a little goes a long way – you want to enhance your subject's natural beauty, not overpower it.

Celebrate Your Macro Masterpieces

As you delve deeper into the world of macro photography, you'll find yourself continually amazed by the intricate beauty and complexity of the tiny creatures that share our world.

So, embrace the adventure, get up close and personal with the wonders of the macro universe, and most importantly, have a blast! After all, as they say in the macro world, "size doesn't matter, it's all about the details."

Camera Settings

Achieving the perfect shot in macro photography is a delicate balance, and camera settings can play a significant role in capturing stunning images of insects and small creatures. Here are some recommended camera settings to get you started:

1. Aperture: A smaller aperture (higher f-number, e.g., f/8 to f/16) will provide a greater depth of field, ensuring more of your subject is in focus. However, this may also require slower shutter speeds or higher ISO settings to compensate for reduced light.

2. Shutter Speed: Aim for a shutter speed fast enough to eliminate motion blur caused by camera shake or your subject's movement. Depending on your lens' focal length and subject's activity, this could range from 1/100s to 1/250s or faster. Using a tripod and remote shutter release can also help you achieve sharp images at slower shutter speeds.

3. ISO: Keep the ISO as low as possible (e.g., ISO 100 or 200) to minimize noise, especially when using a smaller aperture. However, don't hesitate to increase the ISO if necessary to maintain a fast enough shutter speed for sharp images.

4. Focus Mode: Switch to manual focus to have precise control over the focus point on your subject. Autofocus can sometimes struggle with the shallow depth of field and small subjects in macro photography.

5. Drive Mode: Using a single shot or self-timer drive mode can help minimize camera shake. Additionally, consider using a remote shutter release or your camera's self-timer to reduce camera movement further.

6. Image Stabilization: If your lens or camera body has built-in image stabilization, enable it to help counteract camera shake and achieve sharper images.

7. RAW Format: Shooting in RAW format will provide you with more flexibility during post-processing, allowing you to make adjustments to exposure, color balance, and other settings without compromising image quality.

15. A reflection in water or a mirror

Capturing the Magic of Reflections: Mirrors and Water Wonders

Imagine standing at the edge of a serene lake, as the sun casts a golden glow upon the water's surface. Or, picture yourself in front of an antique mirror, witnessing the beauty of a majestic landscape unfolding behind you. It's in these moments that you can't help but feel awe-inspired by the enchanting world of reflections. With just a camera and a keen eye, you can immortalize these magical scenes in a way that would make even Narcissus envious.

Reflections in water or mirrors add a touch of whimsy and depth to your photography, creating images that leave viewers spellbound. Let's dive into the mesmerizing world of reflective photography and discover how you can capture these breathtaking moments.

First, let's begin by understanding the fundamentals. To photograph a reflection, you'll need a reflective surface, like water or a mirror, and a subject. The subject could be anything from a stunning sunset to a charming vintage bicycle. The key is to let your creativity run wild, just like those ducks photobombing your lakeside shots.

When photographing reflections in water, timing is everything. Early mornings and late afternoons offer the best light conditions for capturing those awe-inspiring hues.

Remember, the more still the water, the clearer the reflection. A gentle breeze can turn your mirror-like lake into an impressionist painting. While it's not quite a Bob Ross "happy little accident," it can still produce stunning results.

For mirror reflections, location and angle are vital. Seek out fascinating environments like historic buildings or captivating landscapes.

When positioning your mirror, consider the angle of the reflected subject and the composition you want to achieve. Pro tip: a slight tilt of the mirror can dramatically change the scene, adding a touch of artistic flair.

Now that you've got the basics covered, let's delve into the technical side of things. To get the crispest reflections possible, use a tripod to stabilize your camera and eliminate camera shake.

Additionally, polarizing filters work wonders in cutting through glare and enhancing the colors in your water reflection shots. It's like sunglasses for your camera – who wouldn't want that?

In terms of camera settings, you'll generally want to use a small aperture (higher f-number) to ensure both your subject and its reflection are in focus. If you're feeling adventurous, you can experiment with a shallow depth of field, focusing on the reflection to create a dreamy, ethereal effect. The key is to have fun and let your inner artist take the reins!

Finally, never underestimate the power of post-processing. Photo editing software allows you to enhance the colors, contrast, and sharpness of your reflection shots, transforming a good image into a jaw-dropping masterpiece.

As you embark on your reflective photography journey, remember that practice makes perfect. So, get out there and explore the world of mirrored wonders and aquatic reflections. Unleash your creativity and capture the magic of this enchanting world.

And who knows, you might just become the Ansel Adams of reflective photography!

Camera Settings

While there's no one-size-fits-all approach to camera settings, there are some general guidelines that can help you achieve stunning results when photographing reflections. Here's a list of recommended settings to start with:

1. Aperture: Use a small aperture (higher f-number) like f/8 to f/16 to maintain a deep depth of field, ensuring both your subject and its reflection are in focus. However, if you're going for a more creative approach, you can experiment with a wider aperture (lower f-number) to create a shallow depth of field, focusing on either the subject or the reflection.

2. Shutter Speed: Choose a shutter speed that complements your aperture and lighting conditions. If you're shooting handheld, use a faster shutter speed to minimize camera shake (e.g., 1/60 or faster). For long exposure shots, especially in low light or when using a tripod, slower shutter speeds (e.g., 1/2 to 30 seconds) can help create a smooth, glassy water surface and enhance the reflection.

3. ISO: Keep your ISO as low as possible (e.g., 100 or 200) to minimize noise and maintain image quality. You may need to increase ISO in low light conditions, but try not to go beyond 800 or 1600, as this may introduce significant noise.

4. White Balance: Set your white balance to "Auto" or adjust it to match the lighting conditions (e.g., "Daylight" for sunny conditions or "Shade" for cloudy skies). This will help ensure accurate color representation in your images.

5. Focus Mode: Use manual focus or single-shot autofocus (AF-S or One-Shot AF) to achieve precise focusing on your subject and its reflection.

6. Metering Mode: Choose a metering mode that works best for your scene. Evaluative or matrix metering is suitable for most situations, as it considers the entire frame when determining exposure. However, you can experiment with spot or center-weighted metering to emphasize specific parts of the scene.

7. Shoot in RAW: Capture your images in RAW format to have more flexibility and control during post-processing. This allows you to adjust exposure, color balance, and other settings without compromising image quality.

16. A silhouette against a vibrant background

Photographing Silhouettes: A Vivid Love Affair Between Light and Shadow

Ah, silhouettes! The intriguing love affair between light and shadow that captures the imagination of photographers around the world. This magical combination of contrasting elements creates powerful, striking, and evocative images that leave viewers gasping for more.

So, buckle up, shutterbugs! We're diving into the world of silhouette photography against vibrant backgrounds, where you'll learn to create visual poetry that will make even the most stoic observer swoon.

Now, you might be thinking, "Silhouette photography? That's just shooting a dark figure against a light background, right?" Well, yes, and no. While that's the basic concept, there's a lot more to it than meets the eye. Let's break it down step by step, as we waltz through the tantalizing tango of light, shadow, and color.

First things first: lighting! To capture that perfect silhouette, you need a strong, directional light source that illuminates the background, while leaving your subject in relative darkness.

The sun, our favorite celestial fireball, is perfect for this, especially during the golden hours of sunrise and sunset. These are the times when the sky turns into a canvas, painted with vibrant hues that will make your photos pop like champagne corks at a wedding.

Next up: composition! A great silhouette photograph hinges on the perfect balance of subject, background, and negative space. It's a photographic jigsaw puzzle, where each piece must fit together seamlessly. When selecting your subject, think about its shape and form.
You want a clearly defined outline that's instantly recognizable, even in shadow form. People, animals, trees, and architectural structures all make excellent subjects for this dance of darkness.

Now, let's talk about backgrounds. Remember, we're going for vibrant here! Look for a backdrop that offers a rich tapestry of colors and contrasts. Sunsets and sunrises are fantastic for this, but don't be afraid to get creative. Neon signs, cityscapes, and street art can all make for dazzling backgrounds that will leave your viewers' eyes dancing with delight.

Once you've got your subject and background sorted, it's time to focus on the technical aspects. To achieve that crisp, dark silhouette, you'll need to dial in the correct exposure settings.
A good rule of thumb is to meter for the sky (or background), allowing the camera to naturally

underexpose the subject. This will ensure that your subject is cloaked in shadow, while the background remains a vivacious cacophony of color.

As you play with your camera settings, remember that a fast shutter speed will freeze motion, capturing your subject in sharp relief. A smaller aperture (higher f-stop number) will help maintain a deep depth of field, keeping both subject and background in focus. Finally, keep your ISO as low as possible to minimize noise and ensure a clean, crisp image.

And that, my friends, is the art of photographing silhouettes against vibrant backgrounds! It's a whirlwind romance between light and shadow, where passion and precision come together to create images that will leave your viewers breathless.

So grab your camera, head out into the world, and capture those fleeting moments when darkness and color unite in a passionate embrace. Remember, in the world of silhouette photography, it's always darkest before the dawn... of your next stunning shot!

Camera Settings

To achieve the perfect silhouette photograph against a vibrant background, consider these camera settings as a starting point. However, keep in mind that photography is an art form, and experimentation is key to finding the perfect combination for your specific scene and conditions.

1. Aperture: Aim for a smaller aperture (higher f-stop number) to maintain a deep depth of field, ensuring both your subject and background are in focus. Try settings around f/8 to f/16, depending on your lens and desired depth of field.
2. Shutter Speed: Use a fast shutter speed to freeze motion and capture your subject in sharp relief. Depending on the available light and movement of your subject, start with shutter speeds around 1/200s to 1/500s, and adjust as necessary.
3. ISO: Keep the ISO as low as possible to minimize noise and ensure a clean, crisp image. Start with the base ISO of your camera, usually around 100 or 200, and only increase if absolutely necessary to achieve a proper exposure.
4. Metering Mode: Use spot or center-weighted metering to take a reading from the vibrant background. This will help you properly expose the background while underexposing the subject, creating the desired silhouette effect.
5. Focus Mode: Use single-servo autofocus (AF-S for Nikon or One-Shot AF for Canon) or manual focus to lock focus on your subject, ensuring it remains sharp in the final image.

6. Drive Mode: If your subject is stationary, use single-shot drive mode. If your subject is moving, consider continuous or burst mode to capture multiple frames in quick succession, increasing your chances of nailing that perfect shot.

As you experiment with silhouette photography, you'll discover that subtle changes in lighting, subject, and background can require adjustments to your settings.

So go out, play with your camera, and embrace the joy of discovering the perfect balance of light and shadow!

17. A high-contrast black-and-white image

The Magic of High-Contrast Black and White Photography: A Monochromatic Masterpiece

Lights, camera, action! But wait, what's that? No color? That's right, my fellow photography aficionados! Today, we shall embark on a thrilling journey through the enchanting world of high-contrast black and white photography. So, buckle up and prepare to dive into the monochromatic ocean of visual art!

High-contrast black and white photography, you ask? Well, it's as simple as it sounds: a delightful display of shades, ranging from the darkest black to the purest white.

This magical monochrome palette captures the essence of a scene, stripping it down to its rawest form and highlighting the beauty of contrast, light, and form. It's like your favorite chocolate chip cookie - without the chocolate chips, but still packed with flavor!

Now, let's begin by setting the stage. To create a high-contrast black and white image, you'll need two main ingredients: light and contrast. Say it with me now: "Light and contrast - a match made in monochrome heaven!" These two elements will dictate the final look of your photograph, so play with them like a maestro conducting a symphony!

First, let's talk about light. Direction, quality, and intensity all play a crucial role in shaping the mood of your high-contrast masterpiece. Side lighting, for instance, can accentuate texture and drama, while backlighting might add an ethereal touch. Remember, just like a magician never reveals their tricks, you have the power to manipulate light and create enchanting illusions!

Next up: contrast! High-contrast black and white photography is all about the difference between the lightest and darkest areas of an image. Seek out scenes that feature bold, distinct shades, and watch as the yin and yang of black and white create a tantalizing dance right in front of your lens. The secret sauce here is to experiment with exposure settings to emphasize contrast - because who doesn't like a bit of extra oomph in their photos?

But wait, there's more! To add that extra pinch of pizzazz to your monochromatic masterpiece, consider composition and subject matter. Look for strong lines, intriguing shapes, and patterns that beg to be captured in black and white. Sometimes, it's the simplest things - like the graceful curve of a staircase or the stark silhouette of a tree against a bright sky - that make the most compelling images. After all, it's the little things that count, right?

Now, you may be wondering about post-processing. Fear not, for this is where the true magic happens! Unleash your inner sorcerer and wield the power of editing software to manipulate contrast, brightness, and shadows. Adjusting these elements can turn a seemingly mundane photo into a captivating work of art. The possibilities are endless, so don't be afraid to experiment and let your creativity run wild!

So, there you have it, my fellow photography enthusiasts! The mystical world of high-contrast black and white photography beckons, offering endless opportunities for you to create breathtaking images that will leave viewers spellbound.

Remember, it's all about light, contrast, and a touch of magic - so go forth and capture the enchanting beauty of the monochromatic realm. May your lens be sharp and your contrast be bold!

Camera Settings

To capture the perfect high-contrast black and white image, there isn't a one-size-fits-all solution for camera settings, as different situations call for different approaches. However, here are some general guidelines to help you get started on your monochromatic quest:

1. ISO: Keep it as low as possible (e.g., ISO 100 or 200) to minimize noise and ensure a clean, crisp image. If shooting in low light, you may need to increase the ISO, but be mindful of potential noise.
2. Aperture: Choose an aperture that complements your desired depth of field. For landscapes, you might want a smaller aperture (e.g., f/11 or f/16) to

keep everything sharp. For portraits, a larger aperture (e.g., f/1.8 or f/2.8) can create a pleasing background blur, drawing focus to your subject.

3. Shutter Speed: Select a shutter speed that balances the exposure and captures the desired motion. For handheld shots, use a shutter speed fast enough to prevent camera shake (e.g., 1/60s or faster). To freeze action or capture motion blur, adjust your shutter speed accordingly (e.g., 1/1000s to freeze action, 1/4s or slower for motion blur).

4. Exposure Compensation: Experiment with exposure compensation to emphasize contrast in your image. Overexposing (+1 or +2) can make the whites pop, while underexposing (-1 or -2) can deepen the blacks.

5. Picture Profile/Style: If your camera has a dedicated black and white mode or monochrome picture profile, use it to preview your image in black and white. This will help you better visualize the final result and make informed decisions about exposure and composition.

6. RAW format: Shoot in RAW to ensure maximum flexibility when editing your high-contrast black and white images. This will provide more latitude for adjustments in post-processing, like tweaking shadows, highlights, and contrast.

7. Metering Mode: Use spot or center-weighted metering for scenes with significant contrast to ensure accurate exposure for your subject or the most important part of the frame.

These are general guidelines, and the magic of photography lies in experimentation and adapting to different scenarios.

Don't be afraid to break the rules and let your creative instincts guide you on your monochromatic adventure!

18. A delicious meal or food item

The Art of Capturing Culinary Masterpieces: A Photographic Journey into the World of Food

Foooooooooood! The very sustenance of life, a source of pleasure, and a feast for the eyes. It's no wonder food photography has evolved into an art form in itself.

In this delightful jaunt through the delicious world of culinary photography, we'll explore tips and tricks to help you immortalize your mealtime masterpieces. Are you ready to tickle your taste buds and inspire your inner artist? Let's dig in!

Lights, Camera, Appetite!

Before we embark on our photographic adventure, let's set the stage. Like any great production, capturing a delectable food image requires a bit of pre-planning. Start by selecting the perfect dish, something that makes your mouth water just by looking at it.

It's said that we eat with our eyes first, so choose a dish that will leave your viewers drooling on their keyboards.

Now, let's talk about lighting. Natural light is your best friend in food photography, so make a date with the sun and let it illuminate your culinary creation. Position your dish near a window and watch as the sunlight bathes your food in an ethereal glow. Avoid direct sunlight, though; you don't want your dish to look like it's been cooked twice! Instead, aim for soft, diffused light that highlights the textures and colors of your meal.

Color Me Delicious

The right colors can make or break your food photograph. Imagine a bowl of strawberries on a white plate against a blue backdrop, or a hearty slice of pizza atop a rustic wooden surface.
These color contrasts not only add visual interest but also emphasize the food's natural beauty. So, don't be shy – play with different backgrounds, props, and color combinations to make your dish pop!

The Devil is in the Details

Sometimes, it's the little things that make all the difference. Sprinkle some powdered sugar on those fluffy pancakes or add a sprig of fresh basil to your pasta dish. These tiny details will add depth and interest to your food photos, transforming them from simple snapshots to tantalizing works of art.

And don't forget the power of steam! There's something mouth-watering about seeing steam wafting off a hot dish. Try placing a microwaved cotton ball or a steamy cup of water behind your dish, just out of sight, to create that appetizing effect. The steamier, the better – unless we're talking about rice, of course. In that case, less is definitely more!

Angles, Angles Everywhere!

The right angle can make all the difference between a drool-worthy photo and a dud. Experiment with different perspectives – straight-on, top-down, or even a 45-degree angle. Let your creativity run wild!

Remember, you're the director of this culinary show, so don't be afraid to get up close and personal with your food. Sometimes, the closer, the better. After all, who wouldn't want a macro shot of that glistening chocolate drizzle?

Now that you've got your toolbox of tips and tricks, it's time to dive into the world of food photography. So grab your camera, put on your chef's hat, and get ready to create some mouth-watering memories!
And remember, when it comes to food photography, the only limit is your own imagination – and perhaps the size of your waistband. Bon appétit!

Camera Settings

While the ideal camera settings for food photography can vary depending on your specific camera, lighting conditions, and the look you're trying to achieve, here's a general guide to help you get started:

1. Aperture: A wide aperture (lower f-stop number) like f/1.8 to f/4 is recommended for food photography. This will create a shallow depth of field, keeping the main subject in focus while blurring the background. This helps to draw the viewer's attention to the star of the show - the food!

2. Shutter Speed: Start with a shutter speed of around 1/60 to 1/125 of a second. You may need to adjust it depending on the available light and if you're using a tripod or not. A slower shutter speed will allow more light to enter the camera, but if you're hand-holding the camera, it may introduce camera shake. In that case, stick to a faster shutter speed to avoid blurry images.

3. ISO: Keep the ISO as low as possible to avoid digital noise, which can be distracting and reduce the overall image quality. An ISO of 100 to 400 is generally a good starting point. If you're shooting in low light, you might need to increase the ISO, but be cautious, as higher ISOs can introduce more noise.

4. White Balance: Set the white balance to 'Daylight' or 'Auto' when using natural light. If you're using artificial lighting, such as tungsten or LED lights, adjust the white balance accordingly to ensure accurate colors in your food photos.

5. Focus Mode: Use 'Single Shot' or 'One Shot' autofocus (AF) mode, which locks focus once you half-press the shutter button. This will give you more control over the focus point, ensuring the most important part of your dish is sharp and in focus.

6. Drive Mode: Choose 'Single Shot' drive mode, which takes one photo per shutter button press. Since food photography typically doesn't require capturing fast-moving subjects, this mode will give you the time to carefully compose and capture each image.

7. Image Format: Shoot in RAW format if possible, as it provides more flexibility in post-processing. RAW files capture more data than JPEGs, allowing for better adjustments to exposure, white balance, and color correction in post-production.

The key to great food photography is practice, creativity, and a healthy appetite for experimentation!

19. A busy market or shopping area

Capturing the Magic of Bustling Marketplaces

The bustling marketplace! A cacophony of sights, sounds, and smells that serves as an alluring playground for photographers.

From the vibrant colors of fresh produce to the frenetic energy of shoppers haggling for the best deals, markets and shopping areas are a treasure trove of photographic opportunities just waiting to be discovered.

So, without further ado, let's dive into the enchanting world of market photography and explore how you can master the art of capturing the spirit and vivacity of these thriving spaces.

1.   Embrace the Chaos

As photographers, we often strive for that perfect shot, carefully composed and meticulously arranged. But when it comes to marketplaces, it's time to throw those rules out the window (or at least loosen up a bit). Embrace the chaos!

Allow yourself to be swept up in the whirlwind of activity, and let it guide your lens. The result? Candid moments that truly encapsulate the essence of a busy market or shopping area.

2. The Art of Storytelling

One of the most captivating aspects of market photography is the countless stories unfolding before your very eyes. Each stall owner, shopper, and passerby has a unique tale to tell.

Your job, as a photographer, is to weave these narratives into a visual tapestry. Snap a shot of the old man selling his handcrafted trinkets, or the young couple sharing a laugh over a freshly squeezed juice.

Remember, a picture is worth a thousand words, and a well-captured moment speaks volumes.

3. Patience is a Virtue (and Your Best Friend)

It's tempting to rush through a busy market, snapping away at anything that catches your eye. But in the pursuit of capturing the essence of these bustling spaces, patience is your greatest ally.

Take the time to observe and soak in the atmosphere. Pay attention to the ebb and flow of the crowd, and watch for those fleeting instances that make for truly captivating images. It's like fishing – cast your line, wait, and reel in the perfect shot!

4. Master the Art of Composition

While markets can be chaotic, it doesn't mean your photos have to be. Keep an eye out for patterns, leading lines, and juxtapositions to create dynamic and engaging compositions.

The neatly stacked rows of fruit, the lines of shoppers snaking through the narrow aisles, and the contrasting colors of merchandise are all elements that can transform an ordinary snapshot into a compelling visual narrative.

5. Light Up Your (Market) Life

Lighting can make or break a photograph, and markets are no exception. Early morning and late afternoon sunlight streaming through the stalls creates a warm, inviting atmosphere that's perfect for capturing the spirit of these vibrant spaces.

Don't shy away from the challenge of shooting in low light conditions either – embrace it! Experiment with different camera settings to create images with a moody, atmospheric quality that tells a different side of the market story.

6. Say Hello to Your New Friends

Interacting with the people you encounter in markets can lead to some of the most rewarding photographic experiences. Don't be afraid to strike up a conversation, share a smile, or ask for permission to take someone's portrait. Engaging with your subjects not only adds a personal touch to your images but also helps you develop a deeper connection to the place and its people.

Photographing bustling markets and shopping areas is an exhilarating and rewarding challenge for any photography enthusiast.

By embracing the chaos, honing your storytelling skills, practicing patience, mastering composition, playing with light, and connecting with the people around you, you'll be well on your way to capturing the magic and spirit of these lively spaces. So, grab your camera, head out to your nearest market, and get ready to be inspired!

Remember, the best photographs are often born from a combination of skill, intuition, and a healthy dose of serendipity. With practice and perseverance, you'll find yourself capturing those candid, heartwarming, and enchanting moments that truly encapsulate the essence of market life. And who knows, you might just stumble upon a scene worthy of a frame on your living room wall or a prime spot in your photo album.

Now go forth, intrepid photographer, and seize the day — one vibrant market snapshot at a time!

Camera Settings

While the ideal camera settings for photographing busy markets and shopping areas will vary depending on the specific conditions and your personal style, here are some general recommendations to get you started:

1. Aperture: Use a wide aperture (low f-number) such as f/2.8 or f/4 to create a shallow depth of field. This helps isolate your subject from the background, drawing attention to the main focus of your image. In low light conditions, a wider aperture also allows more light to enter the camera, resulting in better exposure.
2. Shutter Speed: Opt for a fast shutter speed (1/125th of a second or faster) to freeze the action and prevent motion blur. If you want to intentionally capture motion blur to convey the dynamic atmosphere of the market, experiment with slower shutter speeds (1/30th of a second or slower).
3. ISO: Keep your ISO as low as possible (100 or 200) to minimize noise, especially when shooting in bright daylight. In low light conditions or when shooting at faster shutter speeds, you may need to increase your ISO to 800, 1600, or even higher, depending on your camera's capabilities.

4. Focus Mode: Use single-point autofocus (AF-S or One-Shot AF) for stationary subjects or continuous autofocus (AF-C or AI Servo) for moving subjects. This will help ensure your main subject stays sharp and in focus.

5. Drive Mode: Choose single-shot mode for more control over individual images or continuous shooting (burst) mode to capture multiple frames per second, which is ideal for fast-paced situations or when you want to increase your chances of getting the perfect shot.

6. White Balance: Start with the Auto White Balance (AWB) setting, which usually does a decent job of adjusting for different light sources. If the colors in your photos look off, experiment with different white balance presets (e.g., Daylight, Cloudy, Shade) or manually adjust the Kelvin temperature to achieve the desired color balance.

7. File Format: Shoot in RAW format, if possible, for maximum flexibility during post-processing. RAW files retain more detail and dynamic range, allowing you to adjust exposure, white balance, and other settings more effectively than with JPEG files.

You should always adapt the settings to suit the specific conditions and your creative vision.

20. A serene waterscape (e.g., lake, river, ocean)

Serenity Through the Lens: Capturing the Magic of Waterscapes

The sun rises over the horizon, casting a warm golden glow across the rippling surface of a tranquil lake, while the sound of gentle waves lapping at the shore fills your ears. Sound like a dream? Welcome to the enchanting world of waterscape photography!

I'm here to be your guide, sharing the secrets to capturing that perfect shot and immortalizing the beauty of nature. So, grab your camera and let's dive in!

Section 1: Finding Your Perfect Waterscape

The first step in capturing a serene waterscape is finding the perfect location. Whether it's a misty river winding through a lush forest, a secluded ocean cove, or a mirror-like lake reflecting the surrounding mountains, the options are as vast as the ocean itself.

Do some research, ask local photographers or nature enthusiasts, and explore the natural beauty around you. There's no better way to find the perfect spot than getting out there and immersing yourself in nature. Besides, who doesn't love a little adventure?

Section 2: Timing is Everything

Lighting is the key to a captivating waterscape, and in this case, timing is everything. Golden hour, the period shortly after sunrise or before sunset, is a magical time when the sun casts a warm, diffused light across the scene. It's the ultimate recipe for serenity with a side of awe.

Want to add a touch of drama to your scene? Try shooting during the blue hour, the brief window of twilight after sunset or before sunrise. The soft blue light will create an ethereal, otherworldly atmosphere in your photograph, leaving your audience wondering if they've just stumbled upon a portal to Narnia.

Section 3: Equipment Essentials

While you may be tempted to bring an entire photography store with you, capturing a serene waterscape doesn't require a boatload of gear. Here are the essentials:

1. A trusty camera (obviously): DSLR, mirrorless, or even a smartphone – use what you're comfortable with!
2. A sturdy tripod: A must-have for long exposures and sharp, steady shots.
3. Filters: A circular polarizer to eliminate glare and enhance colors, and a neutral density filter for those silky-smooth water effects.

Optional (but highly recommended): A camera remote to avoid camera shake during long exposures, and a lens cloth to keep your glass clean from any sneaky water droplets.

Section 4: Composing Your Masterpiece

A well-composed photograph can tell a story, evoke emotion, and transport the viewer to another world. When framing your waterscape, consider using the rule of thirds or leading lines to draw the viewer's eye through the scene. Look for interesting elements such as rocks, trees, or even wildlife to add depth and context.

Don't forget to experiment with different perspectives! Get low to the ground, or try shooting from a higher vantage point. By mixing things up, you'll create a visual journey that's as refreshing as a dip in the water on a hot summer day.

Section 5: Going with the Flow

Patience, young grasshopper! Capturing the perfect waterscape can require a bit of waiting. Take your time, observe the scene, and embrace the meditative qualities of nature. As the light changes, so will your shot, transforming your image from a mere photograph into a living, breathing work of art.

Embarking on a waterscape photography adventure is not only about capturing stunning images; it's also about immersing yourself in nature, embracing the beauty of the world around us, and finding peace in the process. So, dust off that camera, put on your adventure hat, and set sail for the tranquil waterscapes that await you.

Remember, the journey is just as important as the destination, and with each click of the shutter, you'll be creating memories that last a lifetime.

A great waterscape photograph has the power to transport its viewer to a serene haven, providing a momentary escape from the chaos of everyday life. By following these tips and tricks, you'll be well on your way to mastering the art of waterscape photography and creating images that resonate with and inspire others.

So, go on, let the soothing waves of creativity wash over you, and embark on an adventure that will leave you with a treasure trove of breathtaking waterscape images. And don't forget to have fun along the way – after all, laughter is the best medicine, and a little chuckle on the shoreline never hurt anyone. Now, go forth and capture the magic of serenity through your lens!

Camera Settings

Finding the best camera settings for waterscape photography depends on the specific scene and the desired outcome. However, I'll provide you with some general guidelines to get you started on your journey to capture that perfect serene waterscape:

1. Aperture: A smaller aperture (higher f-number) such as f/8 to f/16 will help you achieve a deeper depth of field, ensuring that both the foreground and background elements of your scene are in sharp focus.

2. Shutter Speed: For capturing the movement of water, consider using a slower shutter speed. For silky, smooth water effects, try a shutter speed between 1-30 seconds. If you want to freeze the motion of waves or splashes, opt for a faster shutter speed, such as 1/250s or faster.

3. ISO: Keep the ISO as low as possible (e.g., ISO 100 or 200) to minimize noise and maintain image quality. You may need to increase the ISO in low light conditions, but try not to go too high to avoid excessive noise.

4. White Balance: Set the white balance according to the lighting conditions or time of day. For sunrise or sunset shots, you might want to choose the "Cloudy" or "Shade" preset to enhance the warm tones. Alternatively, set the white balance to "Auto" and make adjustments in post-processing if necessary.

5. Focus: Use manual focus or single-point autofocus to ensure the focus is precisely where you want it. For many waterscape scenes, you'll want to focus about one-third into the frame to maintain sharpness throughout the image.

6. Drive Mode: If you're using a tripod and a long exposure, set your camera to a 2-second timer or use a remote shutter release to minimize camera shake.

Happy photographing, and may your waterscapes be as serene as a Zen master's garden!

21. An amusement park or carnival

A Whirlwind of Color and Joy: Capturing the Magic of Amusement Parks and Carnivals

Imagine a place where the aroma of cotton candy and popcorn fills the air, where laughter mingles with the mechanical whirring of rides, and where a kaleidoscope of color and light dances before your eyes. Welcome to the enchanting world of amusement parks and carnivals – a veritable photographer's playground!

As you embark on this photographic adventure, let me be your trusty guide, leading you through a wonderland of creative possibilities. Are you ready to immortalize the magic of these delightful destinations? Then strap in and hold onto your camera, because we're about to take a wild ride!

1. The Art of Timing: Seize the Moment

The first trick to capturing the essence of a carnival is to know when to snap that perfect shot. While it's true that a picture is worth a thousand words, timing is worth a thousand pictures. Look for moments of pure joy: children's faces lighting up as they win a prize, a couple sharing a tender moment atop a Ferris wheel, or friends screaming in unison as they plunge down a roller coaster.

Pro tip: Don't be afraid to take a few extra shots – the more the merrier. You never know which one will be the keeper!

2. Savour the Flavors: Food Photography Fun

No visit to an amusement park or carnival is complete without indulging in some mouthwatering treats. Snap a pic of a glistening caramel apple, an expertly swirled ice cream cone, or a fluffy cloud of cotton candy. Make sure to get close enough to capture the scrumptious details – your followers will be able to taste the sweetness through the screen!

Remember: calories don't count at carnivals – but stunning food photos do!

3. Light Up the Night: Mastering the Art of Night Photography

As the sun sets and darkness blankets the park, a new world of photographic opportunities arises. Rides transform into glowing beacons of color, and the atmosphere takes on a mystical quality. Night photography can be tricky, but with a few simple techniques, you'll be illuminating the night like a pro!

To nail those nighttime shots, use a tripod for stability, experiment with slow shutter speeds to capture light trails, and play with different apertures to find the right balance between light and focus. The result? A mesmerizing display of dazzling lights and hypnotic motion.

4. All in the Details: Discovering the Beauty in the Small Things

Amusement parks and carnivals are a treasure trove of intricate details waiting to be discovered. Keep an eye out for whimsical signs, vintage ride designs, and quirky characters that make each park unique. These smaller elements often go unnoticed, but when captured in a photo, they tell a captivating story of their own.

Remember: the devil is in the details, but so is the magic!

5. Creating a Sense of Movement: Embrace the Blur

Carnivals are a whirlwind of activity, and your photos should reflect that energy. Instead of fighting the blur, embrace it! Experiment with panning shots, where you follow a moving subject with your camera while using a slower shutter speed. This technique will render your subject sharp against a blurred background, creating a sense of speed and excitement.

And there you have it! Follow these tips, and you'll be capturing the heart and soul of amusement parks and carnivals in no time. So, grab your camera, gather your courage, and dive headfirst into the swirling chaos of color and joy. Your photographic journey awaits – may it be as thrilling as the wildest roller coaster ride!

Camera Settings

The ideal camera settings for photographing amusement parks and carnivals can vary depending on the specific situation and lighting conditions. However, here are some general suggestions to get you started:

1. **Daytime Photography:**
   - Aperture: f/5.6 - f/11 (to maintain a good depth of field)
   - Shutter Speed: 1/125 - 1/500 (to freeze motion or adjust based on the speed of the subject)
   - ISO: 100 - 400 (to minimize noise in well-lit conditions)
   - White Balance: Daylight or Auto (to accurately represent colors)

2. **Food Photography:**
   - Aperture: f/2.8 - f/5.6 (to create a shallow depth of field and emphasize the subject)
   - Shutter Speed: 1/60 - 1/250 (to avoid camera shake or motion blur)
   - ISO: 200 - 800 (depending on available light)
   - White Balance: Auto or Custom (to accurately represent colors)

3. **Night Photography:**
   - Aperture: f/2.8 - f/5.6 (to allow more light into the camera)
   - Shutter Speed: 1/4 - 30 seconds (slow shutter speed for light trails or longer exposures)

- ISO: 400 - 1600 (increase if necessary, based on lighting conditions)
- White Balance: Tungsten or Auto (to neutralize warm artificial lighting)

4. **Detail Photography:**
- Aperture: f/4 - f/8 (to maintain focus on the subject while blurring the background)
- Shutter Speed: 1/60 - 1/250 (to prevent camera shake or motion blur)
- ISO: 100 - 800 (depending on available light)
- White Balance: Auto or Custom (to accurately represent colors)

5. **Panning Shots:**
- Aperture: f/8 - f/16 (to create a larger depth of field)
- Shutter Speed: 1/15 - 1/60 (slow shutter speed to capture motion blur)
- ISO: 100 - 400 (to minimize noise)
- White Balance: Auto or Custom (to accurately represent colors)

22. A sporting event or action shot

The Thrill of Capturing Motion: Action Shots and Sporting Events

Lights! Camera! Action... in every sense of the word! If photography is your passion, then capturing the thrill and adrenaline of a sporting event or an action shot is the ultimate challenge.

These fleeting moments of sheer athleticism and energy require precision, skill, and a keen eye. But, fear not, my fellow shutterbugs! We're here to guide you through the exhilarating world of sports and action photography, peppered with a few laughs along the way. So, buckle up and let's dive into the race!

First and foremost, let's talk gear. While a fancy camera isn't the be-all and end-all of sports photography, it sure doesn't hurt to have one that can keep up with the pace. A DSLR or mirrorless camera with a fast autofocus system and the ability to shoot at a high burst rate is ideal.

You'll also want a lens with a long focal length, so you can get up close and personal with the action from a safe distance. But remember, it's not the size of the lens that counts; it's how you use it!

Next up: timing. Timing is everything when it comes to action photography, and nailing that perfect shot is like winning the lottery. The key is anticipation: study the sport, know the players, and have a sense of where the action is headed. If you can predict what's about to happen, you'll be ready to press that shutter button at just the right moment. And if you miss it? Well, there's always Photoshop... just kidding! We're purists here, my friends. We take pride in our organic, all-natural action shots.

Now, let's talk about composition. In sports photography, it's not just about freezing the action – it's about telling a story. A well-composed shot can convey emotion, drama, and the intensity of the game.

To achieve this, experiment with different angles and perspectives. Try capturing the athlete's expression, the ball mid-flight, or even the roaring crowd. And don't forget the rule of thirds – because rules are meant to be followed, except when they're not. Sometimes, breaking the mold can lead to the most compelling images.

Ah, lighting – the bane of every photographer's existence. Unfortunately, we can't always control the sun, and indoor lighting can be tricky.

To make the most of available light, crank up your ISO and use a fast shutter speed. This will help freeze the action and minimize motion blur. But if you're feeling adventurous, try playing with slower shutter speeds for a touch of artistic flair. After all, who says a little blur can't be beautiful? Just ask the Impressionists.

Finally, let's address the elephant in the room: patience. Sports photography is not for the faint of heart or the easily discouraged. You may take hundreds, even thousands of shots before you get "the one." But remember, each shutter click brings you closer to perfection.

So, keep practicing, stay focused, and don't be afraid to step out of your comfort zone.

Capturing the essence of a sporting event or an action shot can be an exhilarating and rewarding experience. With the right gear, anticipation, composition, lighting, and a healthy dose of patience, you'll be well on your way to snapping jaw-dropping images that make viewers feel like they're right in the heart of the action.

So, grab your camera, channel your inner sports enthusiast, and let the games begin!

Camera Settings

To capture stunning action shots and sporting events, you'll want to optimize your camera settings for the best possible results. Here are some recommended settings to help you achieve those breathtaking images:

1. Shutter Speed: For freezing motion, use a fast shutter speed. Aim for at least 1/1000th of a second or faster, depending on the speed of the action. You

can experiment with slower shutter speeds if you want to create intentional motion blur.

2. Aperture: A wide aperture (lower f-number, like f/2.8 or f/4) will help you achieve a shallow depth of field, isolating the subject from the background. This setting also allows more light into the camera, which is essential for fast shutter speeds.

3. ISO: Set your ISO according to the lighting conditions. In bright sunlight, a lower ISO (e.g., 100-400) is suitable, while in low-light or indoor situations, you may need to increase the ISO (e.g., 800-3200) to maintain fast shutter speeds without underexposing your images. Be cautious of pushing the ISO too high, as it can introduce noise into your photos.

4. Autofocus: Use continuous autofocus mode (AI Servo for Canon, AF-C for Nikon, or a similar setting for other brands) to track moving subjects and maintain focus throughout the action.

5. Burst Mode: Enable your camera's continuous shooting or burst mode to capture multiple frames per second, increasing the chances of capturing the perfect moment.

6. Metering: Choose a metering mode that best suits the lighting conditions and your subject. For example, spot metering works well for subjects with a significantly different brightness than the background, while matrix or evaluative metering is more suitable for evenly lit scenes.

7. White Balance: Set your white balance according to the lighting conditions or use the auto white balance (AWB) function if you prefer to adjust color balance in post-processing.

8. Image Stabilization: If your lens has image stabilization, turn it on to help minimize camera shake, especially when shooting at slower shutter speeds or with long focal lengths.

23. A local festival or cultural event

Capturing the Magic: A Guide to Photographing Local Festivals and Cultural Events

There's nothing quite like the sights, sounds, and colors of a local festival or cultural event to awaken your inner shutterbug. As a passionate photography enthusiast, let me guide you through the exhilarating world of festival photography, where you'll capture memories and masterpieces that last a lifetime. So grab your camera, embrace your creativity, and let's dive into this visual feast!

1. Know Thy Festival

Before you even think about pressing that shutter button, research your chosen event like a detective on a mission. Understanding the history, traditions, and key moments of the festival will give you the upper hand in anticipating perfect photo opportunities.

Think of it as knowing the secret handshake that opens the door to a world of spectacular images. So hit those books, browse the web, and chat up locals – knowledge is power, my friends!

2. Gear Up, But Keep It Light

While we all secretly yearn for that bat-belt of camera equipment, festivals are not the place to weigh yourself down. Choose your gear wisely, focusing on versatility and mobility. A DSLR or mirrorless camera with a versatile zoom lens (e.g., 24-70mm or 18-135mm) is ideal for capturing both wide-angle scenes and intimate details. Don't forget extra batteries, memory cards, and a comfortable strap. And remember, the best camera is the one you have with you – even a smartphone can work wonders in the right hands!

3. Timing is Everything

The early bird may catch the worm, but the punctual photographer captures the magic. Arriving early to the event not only allows you to scout out prime vantage points but also to soak in the atmosphere and observe people as they prepare for the festivities. You'll be rewarded with candid moments that tell the story of the event like a visual novel.

4. Get Up Close and Personal

Festivals are vibrant, energetic affairs – and your photographs should reflect that! Don't be afraid to step out of your comfort zone and get in on the action. Interact with participants, immerse yourself in the festivities, and capture those raw, unfiltered emotions that make for truly compelling images. Trust me, no one ever won a photography award by playing it safe!

5. Master the Art of Storytelling

Great festival photography is about more than just snapshots of pretty costumes and smiling faces. It's about telling a story, capturing the spirit and essence of the event. Look for images that convey emotions, relationships, and the unique atmosphere of the festival. And don't forget to include context – wide shots of the venue, crowds, and surrounding environment help to create a rich visual narrative.

6. Be Bold with Your Composition

Festivals are the perfect playground for experimenting with creative composition techniques. Play with angles, perspective, and depth of field to create dynamic, engaging images. Frame your subjects with architectural elements or natural features, or use the "rule of thirds" to add balance and interest. And remember, rules are meant to be broken – don't be afraid to push the boundaries and forge your own path in the quest for photographic glory!

7. Keep an Eye on the Light

Light is the lifeblood of photography, and at a festival, you'll be dealing with a smorgasbord of lighting conditions. Whether it's the warm glow of a setting sun, the harsh midday glare, or the neon kaleidoscope of nighttime festivities, learn to work with the light, not against it. Embrace shadows, silhouettes, and backlighting for dramatic effect, and always be prepared to adapt your settings to make the most of the available light.

Photographing a local festival or cultural event can be an exhilarating, rewarding experience that will not only hone your skills as a photographer but also create a treasure trove of memories to cherish.

By understanding the event, choosing the right gear, being mindful of timing, getting up close and personal, mastering storytelling, experimenting with composition, and working with light, you'll be well on your way to capturing the magic of the festivities.

So embrace the excitement, the chaos, and the beauty of it all – and let your photographs tell the story of a thousand words, a thousand emotions, and a thousand memories. Remember, the world is your canvas, and your camera is the paintbrush that brings it to life.

Now, grab that camera, unleash your creativity, and make some photographic magic at your next local festival or cultural event! And who knows, you might even capture a few laughs, gasps, and "wow" moments along the way.

Camera Settings

While there isn't a one-size-fits-all solution for camera settings, as each event and scene may require different adjustments, here's a general guideline to help you get started with photographing local festivals and cultural events:

1. Aperture: Use a wide aperture (low f-number, e.g., f/2.8-f/4) to create a shallow depth of field, isolating your subject from the background and adding an artistic touch. For landscape or group

shots, opt for a narrower aperture (higher f-number, e.g., f/8-f/11) to maintain sharpness throughout the scene.

2. Shutter Speed: To freeze motion and avoid blurry images, use faster shutter speeds (e.g., 1/250s or faster). For nighttime events or capturing intentional motion blur, you may need slower shutter speeds (e.g., 1/60s or slower), but consider using a tripod or image stabilization to reduce camera shake.

3. ISO: Keep your ISO as low as possible (e.g., ISO 100-200) in well-lit situations to minimize noise. In low light conditions or when using fast shutter speeds, you may need to increase your ISO (e.g., ISO 800-3200) to achieve proper exposure, but be aware of potential noise issues at higher ISO levels.

4. White Balance: Set your white balance according to the lighting conditions or use the auto white balance (AWB) setting. For warm, golden light, try the "Shade" or "Cloudy" settings. For artificial lighting, like stage lights or street lamps, try the "Tungsten" or "Fluorescent" settings.

5. Focus Mode: Use continuous autofocus (AI Servo/AF-C) for moving subjects, or switch to single-shot autofocus (One-Shot/AF-S) for stationary subjects. For more control, use manual focus (MF) in tricky situations or when using very shallow depth of field.

6. Drive Mode: Set your camera to continuous shooting (burst) mode to capture fast-paced action or fleeting expressions. This increases your chances of getting the perfect shot in a dynamic environment.
7. Metering Mode: Use evaluative or matrix metering for general scenes, as it takes into account the entire frame. For backlit subjects or scenes with high contrast, consider spot metering or center-weighted metering to ensure proper exposure for your main subject.

As you gain experience and develop your skills, you'll learn to intuitively make the necessary adjustments to capture the magic of the event.

24. A captivating portrait

The Magic of Capturing Souls: A Guide to Captivating Portraits

The art of portrait photography! It's the magical realm where photographers transform ordinary mortals into extraordinary beings, capturing the essence of their very souls.

If you've ever wondered how to weave your own spell and create enchanting portraits, worry no more! We're here to sprinkle some fairy dust on your photography journey and turn you into a portrait wizard.

Picture this: you're in your favorite local coffee shop, and you spot someone with the most intriguing, enigmatic smile. Your fingers itch to snap a photo that will immortalize that very moment.

But how do you go about it? Well, buckle up, because we're about to dive into the world of portrait photography, where we'll explore the secrets to creating breathtaking portraits that will make your audience gasp in awe.

1. Lights, Camera, Emotion!

In portrait photography, lighting is the fairy godmother that can make or break your image. To create a captivating portrait, you need to master the art of playing with light. Soft, diffused light is your best friend – it adds depth and dimension to your subject's features, transforming them into a vision of ethereal beauty.

Natural light is a gift from the heavens, but if you're stuck indoors, fret not! Invest in a good quality reflector or softbox to mimic the natural glow. Just remember, the perfect light is like a good cup of tea – not too strong, not too weak, and with a golden hue that warms the soul.

2. Close Encounters of the Human Kind

Nothing brings a portrait to life like a genuine connection between the photographer and the subject. To capture the true essence of your subject, you need to break down the barriers and forge a bond. Get to know your subject, engage them in conversation, and share a laugh or two (or three). By creating a comfortable and relaxed atmosphere, you'll not only put your subject at ease but also unearth the hidden gems of their personality – the secret ingredient to a captivating portrait.

3. Location, Location, Location

Finding the right backdrop for your portrait is like setting the stage for a grand performance. A carefully chosen location can add depth, mood, and character to your image. Whether you opt for a lush garden, a quirky café, or a graffiti-filled alleyway, make sure your background complements your subject's personality without stealing the spotlight. Remember, your subject is the star of the show – the background is just the supporting cast.

4. Posing with Panache

Ah, posing – the bane of many a photographer's existence. While some people are born with the natural ability to strike a pose, others need a little guidance. And that's where you, the portrait maestro, come in. Direct your subject with clear, concise instructions, and encourage them to experiment with different angles and expressions. And don't forget to have fun! After all, nothing beats the charm of a spontaneous, candid moment.

5. The Eyes Have It

You've probably heard it a million times – the eyes are the windows to the soul. But it's true! In portrait photography, the eyes are the focal point that draws the viewer in, inviting them to unravel the mysteries hidden within. To create a truly captivating portrait, ensure that your subject's eyes are in sharp focus. Play with catchlights – those little reflections of light that sparkle in the eyes – to add depth and life to your image. Remember, the secret to a mesmerizing portrait lies in the eyes, so make sure they speak volumes!

Capturing a captivating portrait is all about connecting with your subject, manipulating light, and paying attention to the little details.

But most importantly, it's about having fun!

Camera Settings

Unleashing the full potential of your camera is crucial to create those mesmerizing portraits. While the "perfect" settings depend on the specific conditions of each shoot, we've got you covered with some general tips to get you started:

1. Aperture: A wide aperture (low f-number, e.g., f/1.8 or f/2.8) helps create a shallow depth of field, which isolates your subject from the background, making them stand out. This also allows more light to enter your camera, which is especially useful in low-light conditions.

2. Shutter Speed: To avoid motion blur, use a fast enough shutter speed. A good rule of thumb is to set your shutter speed at least to the inverse of your focal length (e.g., 1/100s for a 100mm lens). However, if your subject is moving or you're shooting handheld, you may need a faster shutter speed.

3. ISO: Keep your ISO as low as possible (e.g., ISO 100 or 200) to minimize noise and maintain image quality. However, if you're shooting in low-light conditions, you may need to increase your ISO to compensate for the lack of light. Just keep in mind that higher ISOs can introduce more noise, so strike a balance that works for your specific situation.

4. Focal Length: For flattering portraits, opt for a mid-telephoto lens (e.g., 85mm, 100mm, or 135mm).

These focal lengths provide a natural perspective, minimize distortion, and help create a pleasing background blur.

5. Focus Mode: Choose a single-point autofocus (AF-S or One-Shot) mode and focus on your subject's eyes to ensure they are sharp and clear. If your subject is moving, consider using continuous autofocus (AF-C or AI Servo) to track them.

6. Metering Mode: Evaluative or matrix metering generally does a good job of calculating the exposure for portraits. However, if you're dealing with tricky lighting, you might want to switch to spot metering and take a reading from your subject's face.

7. White Balance: If you're shooting outdoors, the "Daylight" or "Sunny" white balance setting should work well. For indoor portraits, "Tungsten" or "Fluorescent" may be more suitable, depending on your light source. Alternatively, you can shoot in RAW format and adjust the white balance in post-processing.

Experimenting with these settings and finding the best combination for your specific shoot is key to creating unforgettable portraits. Remember that photography is an art form, and rules are meant to be broken.

So, go ahead and explore the world of portrait photography, and let your creativity soar!

25. A bird in flight or perched

The Exhilarating Art of Bird Photography: Soaring with Wings and Lenses

Picture this: You're surrounded by the sweet symphony of chirping, the sun gently illuminating the vibrant foliage, and you're about to capture the perfect shot of a bird in flight or perched, like a regal guardian of the skies. If this exhilarating vision stirs your soul, buckle up your camera straps, because we're diving into the thrilling world of bird photography!

First things first, let's talk about the "fowl-weather" friends you'll need: your trusty camera and lens. While any DSLR or mirrorless camera can work wonders, a camera with a fast autofocus and high burst rate will help you snap those birds before they vanish into the air like Houdini. As for the lens, a telephoto zoom (think 100-400mm) or a prime telephoto (such as a 500mm) will get you up close and personal with our feathered friends without scaring them off – unless, of course, you're part avian whisperer.

Now that you've got your gear, it's time to become a bird-watching ninja. Learn the habitat, behavior, and migration patterns of your subjects. You don't want to set up camp in a barren wasteland, only to discover that the bird you're after has booked a one-way ticket to the other side of the globe! Get acquainted with the best spots to find your feathered friends, and be prepared to perch like a pro.

Patience, my dear aspiring bird photographer, is a virtue you'll need in spades. You may have to wait for hours, even days, to witness that magical moment when a bird swoops in and strikes a pose worthy of the cover of "Vogue: Avian Edition." But fear not, for when that moment arrives, it will be worth every tick of the clock.

Now, let's talk technique. When capturing birds in flight, you'll want to use a fast shutter speed (1/1000th of a second or faster) to freeze those rapid wing beats. Combine this with a wide aperture (think f/5.6 or wider) and a higher ISO to achieve a sharp, well-exposed image that will leave your friends and family in awe.

For perched birds, play around with depth of field by using a wider aperture to isolate your subject from the background. This will make your feathered friend stand out like a true superstar. And remember, focus on the eyes – a sharp gaze can make or break a photo, so keep your camera's autofocus point locked onto those mesmerizing orbs.

Composition is key in making your bird photographs truly sing. Keep the rule of thirds in mind, allowing your subject some room to "fly" within the frame. And don't be afraid to experiment – you might just capture that once-in-a-lifetime shot that sends your photography career soaring!

Lastly, have fun and enjoy the process. Bird photography is a magical blend of art, science, and the great outdoors, offering you countless opportunities to connect with nature and create memories that will last a lifetime. So spread your wings, grab your camera, and take flight into the exhilarating world of bird photography. After all, as the saying goes, "A bird in the lens is worth two in the bush!"

Camera Settings

To capture stunning bird photographs, consider the following camera settings:

1. Shutter Speed: For birds in flight, use a fast shutter speed of 1/1000th of a second or faster. This will freeze the motion and give you sharp images. For perched birds, you can use a slower shutter speed (e.g., 1/500th of a second) if the bird is relatively still.

2. Aperture: Use a wide aperture to create a shallow depth of field, which helps to isolate the bird from the background. For birds in flight, consider using an aperture of f/5.6 or wider. For perched birds, you can experiment with even wider apertures like f/2.8 or f/4, depending on your lens.

3. ISO: Set your ISO according to the lighting conditions. In bright sunlight, a lower ISO (e.g., 100-400) is ideal. However, in low light or overcast conditions, you may need to increase your ISO (e.g., 800-3200) to maintain a fast shutter speed and wide aperture.

4. Autofocus: Use continuous autofocus (AI Servo for Canon, AF-C for Nikon, and AF-C or AFC for other

brands) to track the bird's movement. Set a single autofocus point or a small group of points for precise focusing on the bird's eye.

5. Drive Mode: Choose a high-speed continuous shooting mode (also known as burst mode) to capture multiple frames per second. This increases your chances of getting the perfect shot, especially when photographing birds in flight.

6. Metering Mode: Set your metering mode to Evaluative or Matrix (depending on your camera brand), which will consider the entire scene when calculating exposure. This mode generally provides a well-balanced exposure for bird photography.

7. White Balance: Use Auto White Balance (AWB) or adjust it according to the lighting conditions (e.g., Daylight, Cloudy, Shade). You can always fine-tune the colors later during post-processing if you shoot in RAW format.

26. A bustling city street

Capturing the Urban Symphony: A Guide to Photographing Bustling City Streets

The city street: a living, breathing organism that pulses with energy, vibrancy, and life. If you've ever found yourself mesmerized by the urban symphony of honking horns, scurrying pedestrians, and the iconic "taxi!" yell, then you, my friend, have experienced the undeniable allure of city streets.

Now let's explore how to transform that kinetic energy into stunning photographs that capture the essence of urban life.

So grab your camera, lace up your walking shoes, and let's get ready to hit the pavement!

Chapter 1: The Art of Observing
In the immortal words of Ferris Bueller, "Life moves pretty fast. If you don't stop and look around once in a while, you could miss it." The same holds true for photographing city streets.

Before you start snapping away, take a moment to absorb the scene. Watch how the sunlight bounces off glass windows, observe the patterns of movement, and listen to the city's soundtrack. By fine-tuning your senses, you'll develop a keen eye for capturing those fleeting moments that make urban photography so exhilarating.

Chapter 2: Mastering the Technicalities

Now that we've tapped into our inner observer, let's talk technique. From choosing the right camera settings to embracing the nuances of street photography, there's a smorgasbord of technicalities to consider. But don't let that deter you – like a jigsaw puzzle, each piece comes together to form a beautiful picture.

Key ingredients include understanding aperture, shutter speed, and ISO. And while we're at it, let's throw in some compositional techniques like the rule of thirds, leading lines, and juxtaposition. Remember, practice makes perfect, so be patient with yourself and your camera!

Chapter 3: Embracing the Unexpected

In the words of Forrest Gump's mama, "Life is like a box of chocolates; you never know what you're gonna get." The same goes for city street photography. Embrace the unexpected, and let spontaneity guide your lens.

After all, some of the most memorable shots come from serendipitous encounters. Be ready to click at a moment's notice, because, in the urban jungle, you never know when that golden opportunity will arise. So keep your eyes peeled, your camera at the ready, and let the city's surprises come to you.

Chapter 4: Connecting with People

City streets are a melting pot of diverse characters, each with their own unique stories. One of the most rewarding aspects of urban photography is capturing the human element. Whether it's a candid portrait or a staged encounter, remember to approach people with respect and a smile. You might be surprised at the fascinating connections you make and the stories you collect, one click at a time. So go on, strike up a conversation – who knows, you might just make a friend for life.

The Everlasting City Beat

As the sun sets and the city lights start to twinkle, take a moment to reflect on the day's photographic journey. You've ventured through the concrete jungle, embraced the unexpected, and connected with the city's heartbeat. With each frame, you've immortalized a fragment of urban life that will resonate with viewers for years to come. So hold your camera high, and let the world see the bustling city streets through your lens.

After all, you're not just a photographer; you're a storyteller, painting the urban symphony one shutter click at a time.

Camera Settings

Capturing the perfect city street photograph requires an understanding of various camera settings. While there isn't a one-size-fits-all solution, as settings may vary based on specific conditions and desired outcomes, here are some general recommendations to help you get started:

1. Aperture: Use a moderate aperture (f/5.6 to f/8) to balance depth of field and sharpness. This range allows you to keep both your subject and background in focus while maintaining a decent shutter speed. If you want to isolate your subject with a blurred background, opt for a wider aperture (f/1.4 to f/2.8).

2. Shutter Speed: To freeze motion and avoid camera shake, use a faster shutter speed, such as 1/250s or higher. For creative effects like motion blur or light trails, experiment with slower shutter speeds like 1/15s or longer. Just remember that you may need a tripod or image stabilization to avoid camera shake at slower speeds.

3. ISO: Keep the ISO as low as possible (100-400) for optimal image quality and minimal noise. However, if you're shooting in low light or using a fast shutter speed, you may need to increase your ISO to 800, 1600, or higher. Always try to strike a balance between shutter speed, aperture, and ISO to achieve the best results.

4. White Balance: Set your white balance to "Auto" for most situations. However, if you find that your images have an undesirable color cast, try adjusting the white balance manually to better match the scene's lighting conditions.

5. Focus Mode: Use single-shot autofocus (AF-S or One-Shot AF) for stationary subjects and

continuous autofocus (AF-C or AI Servo) for moving subjects. Additionally, select a focus point that best aligns with your subject or intended point of interest.
6. Drive Mode: Set your camera to single-shot mode for precise control or continuous/burst mode if you want to capture a series of images in rapid succession, such as a fast-moving subject.
7. Metering Mode: Evaluative or Matrix metering modes work well for most city street scenarios. However, you might want to switch to Spot metering if you're dealing with tricky lighting conditions or want to emphasize a specific area of the scene.

As you gain experience, don't be afraid to experiment and adapt to the unique conditions of each city street scene.

That's the beauty of photography—making it your own!

27. A starry night sky or astrophotography

Unleashing the Magic of the Night Sky

A serene, moonless night, with nothing but the vast expanse of the cosmos stretched out above you, twinkling stars scattered like a billion tiny diamonds across the dark canvas of the sky.

This, my friends, is the playground of astrophotography. And you, armed with your trusty camera, are about to embark on a spectacular journey to capture the breathtaking beauty of the night sky.

Astrophotography can seem like rocket science, but with a little guidance, a pinch of patience, and a dash of enthusiasm, you'll soon be basking in the glory of your very own celestial masterpieces. So, strap in and let's embark on this cosmic rollercoaster together!

Step 1: The Gear-up

First things first - gear up! You'll need a camera with manual controls, a sturdy tripod, a wide-angle lens (preferably with a fast aperture like f/2.8), and an optional remote shutter release. And, oh, don't forget the warm clothes, a headlamp, and a thermos of hot cocoa - because baby, it's cold outside!

Step 2: The Location Scouting

To capture the stars in all their brilliance, you'll need to escape the clutches of light pollution. So, hop in your UFO (or car, whichever you prefer), and set off in search of the perfect location.

Look for places with minimal artificial light and a clear, unobstructed view of the sky. After all, you don't want any pesky trees photobombing your interstellar masterpiece, do you?

Step 3: The Settings Shuffle

Once you've found the perfect spot, it's time to play around with your camera settings. Set your camera to manual mode, adjust the ISO between 1600 and 3200, and open up the aperture as wide as it goes.

Now, for the pièce de résistance - the shutter speed. Aim for a 20-30 second exposure, but feel free to experiment. Remember, there's no "one-size-fits-all" recipe in the kitchen of astrophotography!

Step 4: The Star-Struck Composition

Now comes the fun part - composing your shot. Use the rule of thirds or the Fibonacci spiral, and try to include an interesting foreground element to add depth and context. Frame your shot so that the celestial wonders take center stage - think constellations, the Milky Way, or even the elusive Northern Lights if you're lucky enough to be in the right spot at the right time. The sky's the limit - literally!

Step 5: The Patient Pursuit

Astrophotography is like baking a soufflé - it requires patience and precision. Once you've composed your shot, click the shutter and wait for the magic to happen. Resist the urge to peek at the preview until the exposure is complete. Trust me, it'll be worth the wait. Just like a fine wine, good things take time - and your starry night sky photo will be no exception!

Step 6: The Post-Processing Party

So, you've got your celestial snapshot in the bag. Now what? Well, it's time to polish that raw diamond and turn it into a shining gem.

Post-processing can help you enhance the colors, reduce noise, and bring out the finer details in your image. Use software like Adobe Lightroom or Photoshop, and remember, subtlety is key - you want your photo to look natural, not like a supernova just exploded in the sky!

And there you have it, folks! A crash course in capturing the wonders of the cosmos through the lens of your camera. So, in summary, astrophotography is a thrilling and rewarding adventure that allows you to immortalize the beauty of the night sky.

By gearing up with the right equipment, finding the ideal location, mastering your camera settings, composing a captivating shot, practicing patience, and refining your image in post-processing, you'll be well on your way to creating stunning celestial masterpieces.

Embrace the journey, revel in the challenge, and let the stars be your muse. As you venture out into the night, remember that the cosmos is your canvas, and you, dear photographer, are the artist.

So go on, unleash your creativity, and let your images of the starry night sky inspire not only you but also everyone who gazes upon them. Because, after all, we're all made of stardust, and there's no better way to celebrate that than by capturing the magic of the cosmos through the art of astrophotography.

Camera Settings

While the ideal camera settings for astrophotography may vary depending on your specific equipment and environmental conditions, here's a general guideline to get you started:

1. Camera Mode: Manual (M) This allows you to have full control over your aperture, shutter speed, and ISO settings.
2. Aperture: Widest possible (e.g., f/2.8) A wide aperture enables you to capture more light, which is crucial when shooting in low-light conditions like the night sky.
3. Shutter Speed: 20-30 seconds A longer shutter speed allows your camera to gather more light, revealing faint stars and celestial details. However, be cautious of star trails forming due to the Earth's

rotation. You can use the "500 Rule" to help determine the maximum shutter speed to avoid star trails: Divide 500 by the focal length of your lens (e.g., 500/18mm = 27.8 seconds).

4. ISO: 1600-3200 Higher ISO values increase the camera's sensitivity to light, which is essential for capturing the dimly lit night sky. Keep in mind that higher ISO values can also introduce more noise to your image, so find the right balance for your camera.

5. Focus: Manual focus set to infinity Autofocus often struggles in low-light conditions, so switch to manual focus and set your lens to the infinity mark (∞) for sharp stars.

6. White Balance: Auto or Daylight (5500K) For most cameras, Auto or Daylight white balance works well for astrophotography. You can always fine-tune the colors during post-processing.

7. Image Format: RAW Shooting in RAW format preserves more image data, giving you greater flexibility during post-processing.

8. Image Stabilization: Turned off Since you'll be using a tripod, it's best to turn off any image stabilization features to avoid introducing any unintended camera movement.

28. A seasonal change (e.g., autumn leaves, snowfall)

Capturing the Magic of Seasonal Change: A Photographer's Guide to Embracing Nature's Transitions

Imagine this: leaves turning into a kaleidoscope of gold and amber hues, the first delicate snowflakes transforming the landscape into a winter wonderland, or spring's arrival with an explosion of color as flowers bloom.

These are the seasonal changes that make our world a constantly evolving canvas, and as photographers, it's our privilege to capture this magical transformation.

In this delightful romp through the seasons, we'll explore tips and tricks to help you immortalize these breathtaking moments and embrace the beauty of nature's transformations.

Autumn Leaves: The Golden Season
Autumn is nature's grand finale, showcasing a vibrant array of colors that would make even a master painter envious. It's the perfect time to put your photography skills to the test and embrace the warm, fiery tones of the season.

Here are a few pointers to help you capture the essence of autumn:

1. Timing is everything: Keep an eye on the local foliage reports, and be prepared to strike when the leaves reach their peak colors. You know what they say: "You can't rush art, but you can definitely miss it!"
2. Experiment with angles: Try shooting from a low angle to emphasize the contrast between the leaves and the sky, or use a telephoto lens to compress the scene and create an impressionist-like tapestry of colors.
3. Make the most of the light: Golden hour (the hour after sunrise or before sunset) is a must for capturing the warm, glowing tones of autumn leaves. The soft, diffused light will make the colors pop and give your images a dreamy, painterly quality.

Snowfall: Winter's Delicate Touch

As the temperatures drop and snow begins to fall, the world is transformed into a serene, monochromatic dreamscape. Embrace the quiet beauty of winter by photographing the delicate details of snowfall. Here's how:

1. Use a fast shutter speed: To freeze the motion of falling snowflakes, you'll need a shutter speed of at least 1/1000th of a second. Faster is better to capture those delightful little icy crystals in all their glory.

2. Overexpose (a little): Snow can fool your camera's light meter, resulting in underexposed images. To counteract this, overexpose your shot by one or two stops to make sure your snow looks pristine and white, not a gloomy gray.

3. Look for contrasts: Snowfall presents a unique opportunity to play with contrasting textures and colors. Seek out bold, colorful subjects against the white backdrop, or focus on the intricate patterns formed by snow-laden branches.

Spring Blooms: Nature's Grand Reawakening

Spring is the season of renewal, a time when the world emerges from its winter slumber and bursts into color. Don't miss the chance to capture this vibrant, fleeting moment in nature's cycle. Here's what to keep in mind:

1. Focus on the details: Get up close and personal with your macro lens to capture the intricate beauty of flowers and buds. Just be sure not to disturb any busy bees – they've got enough on their plate!

2. Play with depth of field: Use a wide aperture to create a shallow depth of field, isolating your subject and drawing attention to the vivid colors and delicate textures of the blooms.

3. Embrace the elements: Don't shy away from photographing spring flowers on cloudy or rainy days. Overcast skies provide soft, even lighting that can bring out the best in your floral subjects, while raindrops can add a touch of sparkle and whimsy.

Capturing the magic of seasonal change is about more than just snapping a pretty picture – it's about embracing the beauty of nature's transformations and connecting with the world around us.

As photographers, we have the unique opportunity to immortalize these fleeting moments, preserving the awe-inspiring spectacle of nature's grand design.

So grab your camera, venture out into the great outdoors, and immerse yourself in the enchanting world of seasonal change. And remember, while practice makes perfect, don't forget to enjoy the process and take the time to appreciate the beauty that surrounds you.

After all, photography is as much about the journey as it is about the destination. Now go forth, capture the magic, and let the changing seasons inspire your creativity!

Camera Settings

The ideal camera settings for capturing seasonal changes will vary depending on the specific conditions and the desired outcome. However, here are some general guidelines to help you achieve stunning results:

Autumn Leaves:
1. Aperture: f/4 to f/11 (depending on desired depth of field)
2. Shutter Speed: 1/60s to 1/500s (depending on subject motion and available light)

3. ISO: 100 to 800 (adjust according to available light)
4. White Balance: Daylight or Cloudy (depending on the weather conditions)

Snowfall:
1. Aperture: f/5.6 to f/11 (to achieve a good depth of field)
2. Shutter Speed: 1/1000s or faster (to freeze the motion of falling snowflakes)
3. ISO: 200 to 1600 (adjust based on available light and shutter speed)
4. White Balance: Auto or Custom (to accurately capture the cool tones of winter)

Spring Blooms:
1. Aperture: f/2.8 to f/8 (for macro photography and shallow depth of field)
2. Shutter Speed: 1/125s to 1/1000s (depending on subject motion and available light)
3. ISO: 100 to 800 (adjust according to available light)
4. White Balance: Daylight or Cloudy (depending on the weather conditions)

Try different settings and review your results to find the perfect combination that brings out the beauty of each season.

29. A long shadow cast by a person or object

Capturing the Elusive Shadow: A Dance of Light and Darkness

You're wandering through a tranquil park just as the sun begins to dip towards the horizon. The golden hour is upon you, and suddenly, you notice a long, ethereal shadow cast by a person or object. An otherworldly beauty in the contrast of light and darkness - it's the perfect photographic opportunity!

Here we dive into the art of photographing long shadows, a realm where the drama unfolds, and imagination runs wild. So, buckle up, grab your camera, and let's ride into the sunset!

Step 1: Timing is Everything
The first rule of shadow photography: it's all about the timing. Long shadows are created when the sun is low in the sky, usually during the magical hours of sunrise and sunset. Keep an eye on the clock, and be prepared to drop everything when Mother Nature calls.
Remember, a true photographer is always chasing light, even if it means sacrificing the occasional dinner date!

Step 2: Gear Up

While you could capture long shadows with any camera, some gear choices will make the process easier and more enjoyable. A wide-angle lens is your best friend when it comes to capturing expansive scenes and dramatic shadows.

It's also helpful to have a tripod to keep your camera steady, especially in low light conditions. And don't forget a dash of patience - sometimes, waiting for the perfect alignment of light and subject can be as exhilarating as watching paint dry (but the results are worth it, trust me!).

Step 3: Compose with Care

Composition is the secret sauce that separates a snapshot from a masterpiece. With long shadows, you want to create a sense of depth and drama, so look for lines and shapes that lead the viewer's eye through the frame.

Try placing the shadow-casting object or person off-center and use the shadow itself as a diagonal or leading line.

And don't forget the Rule of Thirds - even shadows have feelings, and they don't like to be crammed in a corner!

Step 4: Embrace the Contrast

When photographing shadows, contrast is the name of the game. Experiment with exposure settings to emphasize the interplay between light and darkness.

Don't be afraid to let the shadows fall into deep black or the highlights shine with brilliance.

Remember, a little mystery never hurt anyone, and a touch of chiaroscuro can turn your photo into a work of art.

Step 5: Get Creative

Now that you've mastered the basics, it's time to let your imagination run wild. Try capturing shadows cast by people jumping or striking a pose, or experiment with objects to create intriguing shapes and patterns.

Consider using silhouettes to add a layer of mystery and tell a story with your image. And if you're feeling extra adventurous, play with reflections in puddles or windows to create a truly unique perspective. The possibilities are as endless as the shadows themselves!

Photographing long shadows is a delightful dance between light and darkness, where your creativity is the only limit. Embrace the contrast, compose with care, and most importantly, have fun exploring this enchanting realm.

As you venture forth into the world of shadow photography, may your passion for capturing the ephemeral beauty of light never wane. And remember, as photographers, we are the shadow whisperers, always chasing the fleeting embrace of light and darkness.

So go forth and capture those elusive shadows - it's time to make magic!

Camera Settings

To capture the perfect long shadow shot, keep in mind that camera settings can vary depending on your specific situation, including lighting conditions and your creative vision. That being said, here are some general guidelines to get you started:

1. Aperture: Use a smaller aperture (higher f-number) to achieve a deeper depth of field, ensuring both the shadow and the object casting it are in focus. An aperture of f/8 to f/16 is a good starting point.
2. Shutter Speed: Choose a shutter speed that balances the exposure and prevents camera shake, especially if you're shooting handheld. Start with 1/125th of a second and adjust as needed depending on the light conditions. If you're using a tripod, you can experiment with slower shutter speeds.
3. ISO: Keep your ISO as low as possible to minimize noise and maintain image quality. Start at ISO 100 or 200 and only increase it if necessary to achieve the correct exposure.
4. Exposure Compensation: If you want to emphasize the contrast between light and shadows, consider underexposing your shot slightly using the exposure compensation setting (e.g., -1/3 or -2/3 EV).
5. Focus: Use manual focus or single-point autofocus to ensure the focus is exactly where you want it – either on the subject casting the shadow or on the shadow itself, depending on your creative intent.
6. White Balance: Set your white balance to "Auto" or choose the appropriate preset for the lighting conditions (e.g., "Sunset" or "Shade"). Alternatively, shoot in RAW and adjust the white balance in post-processing to achieve the desired look.

7. Drive Mode: Use single-shot mode for static subjects, but switch to continuous or burst mode if you're capturing moving subjects, like people jumping or walking.

30. A rainbow or other atmospheric phenomenon

Capturing the Magic: A Guide to Photographing Rainbows and Atmospheric Phenomena

When nature puts on a show, it's time to grab your camera and become the master of the moment! And what could be more magical than photographing a rainbow or other atmospheric phenomena?

Here, I'll share my passion for capturing these awe-inspiring spectacles and provide you with the know-how to create stunning images that will leave your friends green with envy, or should I say ROYGBIV with envy?

First, let's talk about rainbows – Mother Nature's way of telling us she's a fan of color coordination. Who knew she was such a fashionista? Rainbows are formed when sunlight is refracted, or bent, as it passes through water droplets in the atmosphere. This bending of light creates the stunning spectrum of colors we all know and love. But how do you go about capturing this fleeting phenomenon?

1. **Timing is everything**: Rainbows are all about perfect timing. To catch one, you'll need a mix of sunshine and rain – a sunshower, if you will. Keep an eye on the weather forecast, and when conditions look favorable, have your camera at the ready. The early morning and late afternoon provide the best

lighting for rainbow photography, as the sun's low angle intensifies the colors.

2. **Location, location, location**: Find a spot with an unobstructed view of the sky, ideally away from buildings and trees. Remember that rainbows always appear opposite the sun, so keep your back to the light source. If you're lucky, you might even capture a double rainbow – and no, that's not just a myth!

3. **Choose the right gear**: A wide-angle lens is ideal for capturing the full arc of a rainbow, while a polarizing filter can help enhance the colors and reduce glare. Don't forget a sturdy tripod to keep your camera stable and ensure crisp, clear images.

Now that we've covered the basics of rainbow photography, let's dive into other atmospheric phenomena worth capturing:

A. The ethereal Aurora Borealis: Also known as the Northern Lights, this celestial light show is caused by charged particles from the sun colliding with Earth's atmosphere. To photograph the aurora, you'll need a fast, wide-angle lens and a tripod. Set your camera to manual mode, use a high ISO, and experiment with shutter speeds between 5 and 30 seconds.

B. Dreamy fog and mist: Transform ordinary landscapes into mystical scenes with the help of fog and mist. Early mornings are prime time for fog photography, so set your alarm clock, and don't hit snooze! A longer focal length can help create a sense of depth in foggy scenes, while a tripod will keep your shots sharp.

C. Moody cloud formations: From the wispy cirrus to the imposing cumulonimbus, clouds can add drama and interest to your photos. Use a polarizing filter to enhance contrast, and don't be afraid to experiment with different compositions – the sky's the limit, quite literally!

So, there you have it – a colorful crash course in photographing rainbows and atmospheric phenomena. With a little patience, the right gear, and a healthy dose of enthusiasm, you'll be well on your way to capturing the magic of these natural wonders.
And remember, when it comes to photography, sometimes it's the pursuit of the perfect shot that makes the journey truly unforgettable. Now, go chase that rainbow!

Camera Settings

The ideal camera settings for capturing rainbows and atmospheric phenomena may vary depending on the specific conditions and your camera model. However, here are some general guidelines to get you started:

Rainbows:
1. Aperture: f/8 - f/16 (for a deep depth of field)
2. Shutter Speed: 1/125 - 1/250 (to avoid overexposure)

3. ISO: 100 - 200 (to minimize noise)
4. White Balance: Auto or Daylight
5. Focus: Manual or Single-point autofocus

Aurora Borealis:
1. Aperture: f/2.8 - f/4 (to allow maximum light intake)
2. Shutter Speed: 5 - 30 seconds (to capture the movement of the lights)
3. ISO: 800 - 3200 (depending on the brightness of the aurora)
4. White Balance: Auto or Tungsten
5. Focus: Manual, set to infinity

Fog and Mist:
1. Aperture: f/8 - f/16 (for a deep depth of field)
2. Shutter Speed: Varies, depending on the available light (use a tripod for slower shutter speeds)
3. ISO: 100 - 400 (adjust according to lighting conditions)
4. White Balance: Auto or Cloudy
5. Focus: Manual or Single-point autofocus

Cloud Formations:
1. Aperture: f/8 - f/16 (for a deep depth of field)
2. Shutter Speed: 1/125 - 1/500 (depending on the clouds' movement and available light)
3. ISO: 100 - 200 (to minimize noise)
4. White Balance: Auto or Daylight
5. Focus: Manual or Single-point autofocus

31. A still life of everyday objects

Capturing the Beauty in the Mundane: Still Life Photography with Everyday Objects

Welcome to the wonderful world of still life photography, where the ordinary becomes extraordinary! Put on your creative hat and get ready to experience the magic of transforming everyday objects into mesmerizing works of art.

With a little bit of imagination, some patience, and a keen eye for detail, you'll soon discover that beauty can be found in the most unlikely of places. Let's dive into the exciting journey of capturing still life with everyday objects!

The Art of Seeing

A successful still life photograph begins with a simple yet powerful ingredient: your ability to see. Train your eyes to find the extraordinary in the mundane.

That coffee cup on your desk or the tangled earphones in your drawer can become the stars of your next photography masterpiece. Keep an open mind and let your creativity flow; you never know what gem you might stumble upon.

Composition: Arranging Chaos into Order

Now that you've chosen your subjects, it's time to create a visual symphony through thoughtful composition.

Imagine yourself as the conductor of an orchestra, and your everyday objects are the instruments. It's your job to arrange them harmoniously, so they tell a story or evoke an emotion. Play with shapes, lines, and balance – but remember, sometimes breaking the rules can lead to unexpected brilliance!

Lighting: The Master of Mood

Ah, lighting, the secret sauce of photography! In still life, you have complete control over the lighting, and with that power comes great responsibility. Experiment with different types of light sources, such as window light, artificial light, or even a combination of both.
Observe how light shapes your subject and creates a mood. Embrace the shadows, as they add depth and mystery to your composition. Remember, when it comes to lighting, subtlety is key, and a little bit of finesse goes a long way.

Texture & Color: Add Depth and Flavor

An often-overlooked aspect of still life photography is the attention to texture and color. These elements can elevate a photograph from ordinary to extraordinary. Mix and match different textures and colors to create visual interest and contrast. A colorful book against a rustic wooden background, or a shiny apple sitting on a rough burlap cloth – the possibilities are endless!
Just be cautious not to create a visual cacophony, as it may distract from the true essence of your composition.

Post-Processing: The Finishing Touch

Think of post-processing as the cherry on top of your photographic sundae. With the right amount of editing, you can enhance your still life image, making it truly shine. Adjust the contrast, brightness, and saturation to emphasize your subject, and apply a subtle vignette to draw the viewer's eye. But be mindful not to overdo it, as too much editing can turn your work of art into a "Photoshop nightmare."

The joy of still life photography lies in its simplicity and the boundless creative possibilities it offers. By using everyday objects and a dash of imagination, you can create stunning images that resonate with emotion and beauty.

So, grab your camera, explore your surroundings, and let your creativity run wild. Soon enough, you'll realize that extraordinary moments are hidden in plain sight, just waiting to be discovered by you!

Camera Settings

When photographing a still life with everyday objects, there isn't a one-size-fits-all approach to camera settings. However, I can provide you with some general guidelines to help you get started. Keep in mind that these settings might need to be adjusted depending on your specific subject, lighting conditions, and desired artistic effect.

1. Aperture (f-stop): A medium to small aperture, such as f/8 or f/11, is a good starting point for still life

photography. This will provide you with a larger depth of field, ensuring that most of your subject is in focus. If you want to isolate a specific part of your composition, you can use a larger aperture (smaller f-number) to create a shallower depth of field.

2. Shutter Speed: Since you'll be working with stationary subjects, a slow shutter speed (e.g., 1/30s or 1/60s) should be sufficient. However, if you're using a tripod and want to ensure maximum sharpness, you can opt for even slower shutter speeds. Just make sure that your camera is stable and free from vibrations.

3. ISO: A low ISO value (100 or 200) is recommended to minimize noise and maintain image quality. However, if you're working in low light conditions and need to brighten your image, you may need to increase the ISO. Be cautious not to raise it too high, as this can introduce noise into your photograph.

4. White Balance: Set your camera's white balance according to the light source you're using (e.g., daylight, shade, tungsten, or fluorescent). Alternatively, you can shoot in RAW format and adjust the white balance during post-processing for greater flexibility.

5. Focus Mode: Use manual focus or single-shot autofocus (AF-S or One-Shot AF) to ensure precise focusing on your subject. In still life photography, you typically have the luxury of time, so you can take your time to fine-tune your focus.

6. Metering Mode: Evaluative or matrix metering usually works well for still life photography, as it considers the entire frame when determining the exposure. However, you might need to switch to spot or center-weighted metering if your subject has a very different brightness level from the background.

7. Image Format: Shoot in RAW format if possible, as this will give you greater flexibility and control when editing your images during post-processing.

As always, as you gain more experience and develop your unique style, don't be afraid to experiment and adjust your camera settings to achieve your desired artistic vision.

32. A macro shot of a water droplet or dew

Magnifying Life: Capturing the Magic of Water Droplets and Dew in Macro Photography

The tiny, glistening droplet of dew delicately poised on a blade of grass, reflecting a world full of wonder and enchantment.

In the vast expanse of nature, this small, transient gem can easily be overlooked.

However, with the magical touch of macro photography, we can unlock the hidden beauty of water droplets and dew, transforming them into mesmerizing works of art.

So grab your camera, pull up your rubber boots, and let's explore this fascinating world together!

1. **Gearing Up for the Tiny Wonders**: To capture the delicate intricacies of water droplets and dew in macro photography, you'll need some essential equipment. First and foremost, a good macro lens is a must-have – something with a 1:1 magnification ratio to truly bring those droplets to life.

    Tripods are also essential to ensure the stability required for those crisp, clear shots.

    Don't forget a cable release or wireless remote to prevent camera shake when pressing the shutter button – or you can always use the timer function if you're feeling a bit more old-school.

2. **The Early Bird Gets the Dew**: Ah, the joys of waking up early! The world is peaceful, the air is fresh, and you're half-asleep, wondering why on earth you're doing this. But when you see the first glimmer of sunlight illuminating those dewdrops like nature's own fairy lights, you'll know it was worth it.

   Early morning is the prime time to find dew and water droplets at their freshest, so set your alarm and embrace the magic of dawn.

3. **Composing a Masterpiece**: Once you've found the perfect droplet or dew, it's time to get creative with composition. Experiment with different angles and perspectives to capture reflections within the droplet, or use the rule of thirds to make your subject shine.

   Depth of field also plays a crucial role in macro photography; a shallow depth of field can isolate your subject and create a dreamy, ethereal background, while a deeper depth of field can emphasize the intricate patterns and textures of the surrounding environment.

4. **Light it Up**: When it comes to illuminating your dewy subjects, the sun is your best friend – and sometimes your frenemy. While natural light can create stunning effects, it can also be unpredictable and harsh. To counteract this, try using a diffuser to soften the light, or a reflector to bounce it back onto your subject.

Don't be afraid to get creative with artificial light sources, like ring lights or LED panels, to bring your droplet-filled world to life.

5. **Patience, Young Grasshopper**: Macro photography is not for the faint of heart, and capturing the perfect water droplet or dew requires oodles of patience. You'll find yourself waiting for the wind to subside, or contorting your body into strange positions to get the perfect shot.
   Embrace the challenges, and remember, the journey is half the fun! As a wise photographer once said, "In macro photography, you don't take the shot, the shot takes you."

Capturing the intricate beauty of water droplets and dew in macro photography is a thrilling and rewarding adventure. It requires patience, creativity, and a willingness to embrace the smaller wonders of life.
So get out there, gear up, and start magnifying the magic of the world around you – one tiny, glistening droplet at a time.

Camera Settings

To capture stunning macro shots of water droplets and dew, you'll want to dial in the optimal camera settings for your specific environment and subject. Here's a guideline to get you started:

1. Aperture: Use a moderately wide aperture to achieve a shallow depth of field and isolate your subject. Start with an aperture setting between f/2.8 and f/5.6, and adjust as needed for your desired depth of field. If you want more of your subject and surroundings in focus, opt for a smaller aperture, such as f/8 or f/11.

2. Shutter Speed: A fast shutter speed is essential to freeze motion, especially if you're dealing with a slight breeze that may cause your subject to move. Start with a shutter speed of 1/125s or faster, depending on the available light. If you're using a tripod and there's no wind, you can experiment with slower shutter speeds.

3. ISO: Keep the ISO as low as possible to minimize noise and maintain image quality. Start with an ISO of 100 or 200 and adjust upward only if necessary to achieve the correct exposure. If you're using artificial light or shooting in bright daylight, a low ISO should suffice.

4. Focus Mode: Set your camera to manual focus (MF) or autofocus with manual override (AF+MF). Macro photography often requires precise focusing, and manual adjustments allow you to fine-tune the focus point to ensure the sharpest image.

5. Drive Mode: Use single-shot mode or set a 2- or 10-second timer to minimize camera shake when pressing the shutter button. Alternatively, use a cable release or wireless remote to trigger the shutter without physically touching the camera.

6. Image Stabilization: If your camera or lens has built-in image stabilization, be sure to enable it when shooting handheld to reduce the risk of motion blur. If you're using a tripod, consider turning off image stabilization, as it can sometimes introduce blur when the camera is already steady.

7. RAW Format: Shoot in RAW format to retain the most information and enable greater flexibility during post-processing. This allows you to make adjustments to exposure, white balance, and other settings without degrading the image quality.

33. A local artisan at work (e.g., glassblower, barista, blacksmith)

Capturing the Soul of Craftsmanship: A Journey Through Artisan Photography

Framing the Master at Work

There's no greater thrill for a photography enthusiast than capturing the raw essence of a skilled artisan in the throes of their craft.

Picture this: the focused gaze of a glassblower, sweat trickling down their brow, as they masterfully shape molten glass; the deft hands of a barista creating intricate latte art; or the powerful strikes of a blacksmith against glowing metal.

Each scene tells a story, and as photographers, it's our mission to immortalize these moments with the click of a shutter. This photographic escapade is about discovering the nuances of local artisans at work, sharing their passion, and crafting visual masterpieces.

Step 1: Preparation – The Key to Crafting the Perfect Shot

As the saying goes, "Failing to prepare is preparing to fail." And we don't want that, do we? Researching your subject is an essential first step in the artisan photography process. Understanding the intricacies of their craft will allow you to anticipate key moments, spot unique details, and ultimately capture the artisan's passion in a single frame. So grab your trusty notepad, channel your inner Sherlock Holmes, and learn all you can about the artisan's work!

Step 2: Building Rapport – The Magic Ingredient

Next up, we're going to talk about the secret sauce to making your artisan photography journey unforgettable: building rapport. Like a dance, photography is a collaborative experience between the subject and the photographer.

Taking the time to connect with the artisan, share your intentions, and express your genuine interest in their work can make all the difference. After all, who doesn't want to be the muse to a modern-day Ansel Adams?

Step 3: Capturing the Essence – The Art of Composition and Timing

Now that you've done your homework and forged a connection with the artisan, it's time to put your photographic prowess to work. Keep an eye out for those decisive moments that capture the essence of the artisan's craft.

For instance, the instant a blacksmith's hammer meets the glowing metal, or the delicate moment a barista finishes the last flourish on a latte. Timing is everything – but so is composition. Experiment with angles, depth of field, and lighting to create a visual narrative that does justice to the artisan's dedication.

Step 4: The Big Reveal – Sharing Your Art with the Artisan

You've captured the soul of craftsmanship, and it's time to share your art with the world! Or, at the very least, with the artisan who inspired it. Sharing your work with the artisan can be a profoundly gratifying experience.

It's an opportunity to express your gratitude for their time, showcase your talent, and revel in the magic you've created together. Who knows, they might even invite you back for a masterclass in their craft!

A Celebration of Passion and Talent

In the end, photographing a local artisan at work is about more than just snapping a pretty picture. It's a celebration of passion, talent, and the human spirit.

By connecting with these skilled artisans and capturing their craft, you not only create stunning images but also help to share and preserve their art for future generations. So go forth, intrepid photographer, and capture the beauty of craftsmanship with every click of your shutter – and remember, a picture is worth a thousand words, but the memories are priceless.

Camera Settings

The optimal camera settings for photographing local artisans at work will vary depending on factors such as lighting conditions, the type of craft being captured, and the photographer's artistic vision. However, here are some general guidelines to help you achieve stunning results:

1. Aperture: A wide aperture (low f-number) is generally preferred, as it creates a shallow depth of field that isolates the subject and draws attention to the artisan and their work. Consider using an aperture between f/1.8 and f/4, adjusting as needed based on the desired depth of field and available light.

2. Shutter Speed: Choose a shutter speed fast enough to freeze the artisan's movement, especially if you're capturing fast-moving crafts such as glassblowing or blacksmithing. A shutter speed of 1/125th to 1/250th of a second is a good starting point. If you'd like to emphasize motion blur for artistic effect, experiment with slower shutter speeds.

3. ISO: To achieve the best image quality, keep the ISO as low as possible while maintaining a proper exposure. Start with an ISO of 100 or 200 and adjust as necessary based on lighting conditions. If shooting indoors or in low light, you may need to increase your ISO to 800 or even 1600.

4. White Balance: Accurate color representation is essential when capturing the artistry of local artisans. Set your camera's white balance to match the dominant light source in the scene, or use custom white balance for the most accurate results.

5. Focus: Use single-point autofocus to ensure that the focus is precisely on the artisan or the area of their work you want to emphasize. For moving subjects, consider using continuous autofocus (also known as AI Servo or AF-C, depending on your camera brand) to track the subject's movement and maintain focus.

6. Drive Mode: Shooting in single-shot mode works well for most artisan photography situations. However, if you're capturing fast-paced action, consider using continuous shooting mode (burst mode) to increase your chances of capturing the perfect moment.

7. Image Stabilization: If your camera or lens has image stabilization, enable it to help reduce the risk of camera shake, especially when shooting handheld in low light or with slower shutter speeds.

8. RAW vs. JPEG: Shooting in RAW format provides more flexibility in post-processing, allowing you to fine-tune exposure, white balance, and other settings to create the perfect final image. However, if you prefer minimal editing, JPEG may be the way to go.

34. A panoramic view

Capturing the World in a Frame: Panoramic Photography for Everyone

A Wide, Wide World of Wonder

Ladies and gentlemen, boys and girls, gather 'round and prepare to be dazzled by the wonders of panoramic photography!

Yes, dear reader, today we shall embark on a thrilling journey to master the art of capturing those jaw-dropping, wide-angled, awe-inspiring views that make our beautiful planet a visual feast for the eyes.

So, grab your trusty camera, and let's dive into the world of panoramas. Ready, set, click!

Chapter 1: It's All About Perspective (Wink, Wink)

Now, you might be wondering, "What exactly is a panoramic photo?" Well, imagine squeezing the majesty of the Grand Canyon or the vast expanse of the African savannah into a single frame.

A panorama is simply a wide-angled image that showcases the grandeur of a scene in all its glory. Think of it as a photograph with a little extra "oomph" – like adding hot sauce to your favorite dish. Delicious!

Chapter 2: The Equipment: Your Panoramic Arsenal

Fear not, aspiring panoramic photographer, for you don't need to mortgage your house to invest in the latest high-end camera gear. In fact, many smartphones today come equipped with built-in panoramic features.

However, if you're aiming for top-notch quality, consider investing in a DSLR or mirrorless camera, a wide-angle lens, and a tripod for stability.

Trust me, your panoramas will be so stunning that you'll want to wrap your living room walls in them!

Chapter 3: The Technique: Making It Click (Literally)

Ah, we've reached the exciting part! Now, let's get those creative juices flowing and learn how to create panoramas that would make even Ansel Adams swoon. Here are a few tips to get you started:

1. Scout your location: The perfect panorama starts with the perfect spot. Look for places that offer sweeping vistas and minimal obstructions. Think mountaintops, beaches, or city skylines.

2. Level up: A wonky horizon can make your panorama look like a Picasso painting gone wrong. Use your tripod and a bubble level to ensure your camera is, well, on the level.

3. Overlap for success: When shooting multiple images to stitch together later, overlap each frame by about 30%. This will make merging the images a piece of cake – and who doesn't like cake?

4. Stay steady: Use a remote shutter release or your camera's self-timer to minimize camera shake. The sharper the images, the better the final panorama.

5. Shoot RAW: For the best results, shoot in RAW format. This will allow you to make adjustments during post-processing without compromising image quality.

Chapter 4: Stitching It Together: Where the Magic Happens

Now that you've captured your breathtaking images, it's time to create your panorama. There are numerous software options available for stitching images together, such as Adobe Lightroom or PTGui. Simply import your photos, let the software work its magic, and voilà – you've got yourself a captivating panorama that's bound to make your friends and family green with envy!

Embracing the Panoramic Possibilities

Congratulations, dear reader! You've just dipped your toes into the wondrous world of panoramic photography. As you explore this art form, remember that practice makes perfect – or, in our case, practice makes panoramas.

So, go on, venture into the great outdoors, and unleash your inner artist. The world is your canvas, and it's time to capture it in all its panoramic glory!

Camera Settings

Ah, the nitty-gritty of camera settings! While the best settings may vary depending on your specific camera model, the lighting conditions, and your artistic vision, here's a general guide to get you started on your panoramic photography adventure:

1. Aperture: Use a smaller aperture (larger f-number) like f/8 to f/16 to achieve a greater depth of field, ensuring both the foreground and background are in focus.
2. Shutter Speed: Choose a shutter speed that works well with your chosen aperture and lighting conditions. If you're shooting handheld, make sure it's fast enough to avoid camera shake (e.g., 1/60s or faster). If using a tripod, you can experiment with longer exposures.
3. ISO: Keep the ISO as low as possible (e.g., 100 or 200) to minimize image noise. If you're shooting in low light, you may need to increase the ISO, but be mindful of the trade-off between higher ISO and increased noise.
4. Focus: Switch to manual focus and set the focus at the hyperfocal distance – the point where everything from half that distance to infinity appears sharp. This will ensure maximum sharpness throughout your panorama.
5. White Balance: Set the white balance manually (e.g., daylight, cloudy, etc.) to ensure consistent

colors across all the images you'll be stitching together. Using the auto white balance might result in varying colors between frames.

6. Image Format: Shoot in RAW format to have more flexibility and control during post-processing.
7. Exposure Mode: Use Manual (M) mode to maintain consistent exposure settings throughout all the shots in your panorama.
8. Metering Mode: Set your camera to matrix or evaluative metering mode to obtain a balanced exposure across the entire scene.

Experimenting with different settings is part of the joy of photography, so feel free to tweak these recommendations to achieve the results you desire. Embrace the journey, and may your panoramas be nothing short of spectacular!

35. A piece of abstract art

Capturing the Intangible: A Dive into Abstract Art Photography

Imagine standing before a canvas that transcends the boundaries of reality, a whirlwind of colors and shapes that seem to dance before your eyes. This, my friends, is the exhilarating world of abstract art!

In this thrilling roller coaster of a journey, we'll dive into the realm of photographing abstract art, exploring techniques and tips that will make your inner shutterbug squeal with delight.

First, let's address the question that might be lingering in your mind: "Why photograph abstract art?" Well, dear reader, the answer lies in the captivating essence of abstraction itself. It's a realm where anything is possible, where your creativity can soar to the farthest reaches of the cosmos.

Photographing abstract art allows you to capture and convey emotions, thoughts, and ideas that traditional photography might struggle to express. It's like unleashing your inner Picasso with the power of a camera!

Now that we've established the "why," let's dive into the "how." Here are some tips and tricks to transform your abstract art photography from a bland bowl of oatmeal to a vibrant, spicy curry that'll leave your audience craving more:

1. Embrace the distortion: Don't be afraid to twist and turn your perspective to create a new, exciting reality. Experiment with different angles, lenses, and viewpoints to bring out the magical allure of your subject. Remember, in abstract photography, "normal" is just a setting on a washing machine!

2. Play with focus: The sharpness of your subject isn't always the main attraction. Use selective focus, or even intentional blur, to create dreamy, ethereal images that'll have your audience questioning the very fabric of reality. A little bit of blur never hurt anyone – except maybe those who've misplaced their glasses.

3. Light it up: The right lighting can turn an ordinary scene into an extraordinary work of art. Play with shadows, highlights, and colors to create a visual symphony that makes your abstract art sing. After all, a well-lit piece of art is like a perfectly toasted marshmallow – golden, delightful, and impossible to resist.

4. Get up close and personal: Sometimes, the most intriguing aspects of abstract art lie in the tiniest details. Don't be afraid to get up close and personal with your subject. Capture the brushstrokes, the textures, and the intricate patterns that make your subject truly unique. It's like being an art detective, but with a camera instead of a magnifying glass!

5. Post-processing prowess: Your creative journey doesn't end when you press the shutter button. The digital darkroom is your playground, where you can enhance colors, manipulate shapes, and add your own artistic flair to your images. Just remember, with great power comes great responsibility – use your editing skills wisely, young Padawan.

Now that you're armed with these tips and tricks, you're ready to embark on your abstract art photography adventure. Remember, the sky's the limit when it comes to creativity, and in this wondrous realm of abstraction, the only boundaries are the ones you set for yourself.
So grab your camera, channel your inner Monet, and get ready to capture the intangible – one mesmerizing click at a time!

Camera Settings

When it comes to photographing abstract art, there isn't a one-size-fits-all approach to camera settings. However, here's a list of suggested starting points that can serve as a foundation for your creative experimentation:

1. Aperture: A wide aperture (low f-number) can help create a shallow depth of field, isolating your subject from the background and emphasizing the abstract elements. Conversely, a narrow aperture (high f-number) can keep more of the scene in focus, which may be ideal for capturing intricate details and

textures. Experiment with apertures in the range of f/1.8 to f/11.

2. Shutter Speed: Depending on your desired outcome, you may want to use a fast shutter speed (1/250s or faster) to freeze motion and maintain sharpness, or a slower shutter speed (1/30s or slower) to introduce intentional blur and movement. For handheld shooting, remember to adhere to the reciprocal rule to avoid camera shake.

3. ISO: As a general rule, start with the lowest ISO setting available on your camera (usually around ISO 100) for minimal noise and optimal image quality. Increase the ISO only when necessary to achieve the desired exposure or to compensate for low light conditions, while keeping an eye on noise levels.

4. Focus Mode: Manual focus can give you full control over the focus point, allowing you to experiment with selective focus and intentional blur. Alternatively, use autofocus with a single or flexible spot focus point to quickly and accurately lock onto your desired subject.

5. White Balance: Experiment with different white balance settings to capture the true colors of the artwork or to creatively alter the color temperature for a unique interpretation. You can also shoot in RAW format to have more flexibility in adjusting white balance during post-processing.

6. Metering Mode: Start with Matrix or Evaluative metering to achieve a balanced exposure, and then experiment with Center-weighted or Spot metering

to account for specific lighting conditions or creative intentions.

7. Drive Mode: Single shot or continuous shooting modes can both be useful, depending on whether you're capturing a static scene or incorporating motion into your abstract art photography.

The beauty of abstract art photography lies in your ability to experiment, play, and discover the settings that best complement your creative vision.
Don't be afraid to break the rules and push your camera to its limits – you might just stumble upon a mesmerizing masterpiece!

36. A vibrant sunset or sunrise through trees

Capturing the Essence of Dawn and Dusk: A Journey through Light and Shadows

The allure of a breathtaking sunrise or a mesmerizing sunset! Few sights can rival the sheer beauty and dramatic splendor of these celestial spectacles. Now, picture the scene: a golden orb of light rising or setting amidst a silhouette of majestic trees, their branches reaching out like nature's dancers on the stage of life.

This, my friends, is a moment that every photography enthusiast should aspire to capture! So, grab your camera, join me on this adventure, and together, let's learn how to immortalize those vibrant sunrises and sunsets through the trees.

First, let's talk about the "when." Timing is everything when it comes to capturing the perfect shot. For sunrises, you'll want to be an early bird (you know what they say: the early photographer catches the sun!). Keep an eye on the weather forecast and scout out the ideal location the day before.

Sunsets, on the other hand, require a little less sleep sacrifice, but you'll still want to be at your chosen spot in good time to set up your equipment and soak in the atmosphere.

Once you've figured out the perfect time and place, it's all about mastering the interplay of light and shadow. This is the moment where you can let your artistic instincts run wild.

Use the trees as a natural frame, and play with different angles to create contrast and depth in your composition. The trees can act as a bold, dark foreground that emphasizes the vivid colors of the sky, or they can serve as a softer, more ethereal frame that invites the viewer to explore the scene further.

Now, let's discuss the nitty-gritty technicalities. To capture the full range of colors and light, you'll want to experiment with different camera settings.
Aperture, shutter speed, and ISO all play crucial roles in getting that perfect shot. A smaller aperture (higher f-number) will create a sharper focus throughout the scene, while a slower shutter speed will allow more light to enter, capturing the subtle nuances of the sky's colors.
Don't be afraid to play around with these settings, as finding the perfect balance is key to creating a visually striking image.

One pro tip: consider using a tripod to stabilize your camera. This will not only minimize the risk of blurry images caused by camera shake, but also allow you to experiment with longer exposures, which can yield truly magical results.

Imagine a scene where the last light of day paints the sky in soft, pastel hues, while the trees stand like silent sentinels guarding the entrance to a dreamworld. That's the kind of enchantment a tripod can help you achieve!

As you embark on your quest to capture the perfect sunrise or sunset through trees, don't forget that, ultimately, photography is about storytelling. Each image is a reflection of your unique perspective and creativity, so allow your imagination to take flight.

Embrace the unexpected, find joy in the fleeting moments, and let your photos be a celebration of the beauty that surrounds us. Remember, the most captivating photographs are not merely about technique, but about the heart and soul that you pour into them.

So, gather your gear, venture into the great outdoors, and let the sun's first or last rays guide you on your path to photographic glory. And who knows? You might just stumble upon a scene that leaves you breathless, with a click of the shutter that tells a story worth a thousand words.

Camera Settings

While the ideal camera settings for photographing a vibrant sunrise or sunset through trees can vary depending on the specific lighting conditions, your chosen composition, and your creative vision, here are some general guidelines to get you started:

1. Aperture: Use a smaller aperture (higher f-number) to achieve a deeper depth of field, keeping both the trees and the sky in focus. Consider starting with an aperture setting of f/8 to f/16.
2. Shutter Speed: Begin with a shutter speed of around 1/60 to 1/125 seconds, depending on the available light. If you're using a tripod and want to experiment with longer exposures, you can try shutter speeds of several seconds or even longer, depending on your desired effect.
3. ISO: Keep your ISO as low as possible to reduce noise and maintain image quality. Start with an ISO of 100 or 200, and increase it only if necessary to achieve a proper exposure.
4. White Balance: For a natural look, set your white balance to "Daylight" or "Auto." However, if you want to enhance the warm tones in your image, try using the "Cloudy" or "Shade" white balance settings.
5. Exposure Compensation: If you find that your images are too dark or too bright, adjust the exposure compensation accordingly. Start with 0 EV and increase or decrease it in small increments (e.g., +/- 1/3 EV or +/- 1/2 EV) until you achieve the desired exposure.

6. Focus: Use manual focus or single-point autofocus to ensure that your camera focuses precisely on the part of the scene you want to be sharp. For scenes with both foreground and background elements, like trees and the sky, consider focusing on a point approximately one-third into the frame to maximize overall sharpness.

7. Shoot in RAW: To have the most flexibility in post-processing and to capture the widest range of colors and details, shoot in RAW format.

37. A spiral staircase or unique architectural element

The Art of Capturing the Swirling Majesty: Spiral Staircases and Unique Architectural Wonders

From the moment you lay your eyes on a mesmerizing spiral staircase or an awe-inspiring architectural marvel, you can't help but feel a shiver of excitement.

These twisting, turning flights of fancy aren't just functional structures - they're visual symphonies, a dance of lines and curves that can leave even the most seasoned photographer giddy with delight.

So buckle up, shutterbugs, because we're about to embark on a whirlwind tour of tips and tricks for capturing these enchanting edifices in all their hypnotic splendor.

Step 1: Find Your Muse

A building is like a fine wine – you can't fully appreciate it until you take a moment to savor its nuances. Take a leisurely stroll around the structure, letting your eyes drink in every curve and contour.

Once you find that perfect angle that makes your heart sing (and your camera tremble with anticipation), it's time to set up shop.

Step 2: Embrace the Geometry

When it comes to spiral staircases, the geometry is the star of the show. Whether you're working with a tight helix or a languid curve, the lines and angles are your bread and butter. Use leading lines to draw the viewer's eye into the image, and experiment with different perspectives to make those shapes pop. Remember, a change in perspective can turn a mundane staircase into a mathematical masterpiece!

Step 3: Let There Be Light (But Not Too Much)

Ah, light – the fickle friend of every photographer. To capture the true essence of a spiral staircase or an architectural wonder, you'll want to harness the power of natural light. But beware: too much light can wash out your image, while too little can leave it shrouded in mystery (and not in a good way).

Wait for the golden hour, when the sun's rays are soft and diffused, to really make those architectural elements shine.

Step 4: Composition is Key

When photographing staircases and unique structures, it's all about balance. A well-composed shot is like a perfectly arranged plate of hors d'oeuvres: you want a little bit of everything, but not too much of any one thing.

Experiment with the rule of thirds and other compositional techniques to create an image that's visually satisfying, and don't be afraid to break the rules if it feels right. As the old saying goes, rules are meant to be... gently bent in the name of artistic expression.

Step 5: Take Your Time

Photographing architectural marvels is not a sprint; it's a marathon. Be patient and take your time to explore different angles, settings, and compositions. Remember,

Rome wasn't built in a day, and neither are your best shots. So take a deep breath, slow down, and let the magic unfold before your very eyes.

Step 6: Edit with Love

The perfect shot is rarely achieved straight out of the camera. A little post-processing love can go a long way in bringing out the true beauty of your architectural muse. Play with contrast, saturation, and sharpness to make those lines and curves sing, but don't go overboard – you want to enhance the image, not drown it in a sea of filters.

And there you have it! With these tips and tricks in your photography toolbox, you're ready to embark on your own architectural odyssey. Just remember to keep an open mind, stay curious, and above all, have fun. After all, the world is your staircase – so get out there and start climbing!

Camera Settings

Capturing the enchanting beauty of a spiral staircase or a unique architectural element requires careful consideration of camera settings.
While the ideal settings will vary depending on the specific conditions and the photographer's artistic vision, the following recommendations serve as a solid starting point:

1. Aperture (f-stop): To ensure sharpness throughout the frame, opt for a narrower aperture. An aperture

in the range of f/8 to f/16 should provide a sufficient depth of field for most architectural subjects.

2. Shutter Speed: Choose a shutter speed that complements the available light and the stability of your camera. When shooting handheld, use a speed that's at least as fast as the inverse of your focal length (e.g., 1/50s for a 50mm lens) to minimize camera shake. If using a tripod, you can experiment with longer shutter speeds, allowing for lower ISO settings and less noise.

3. ISO: To maintain image quality, aim for the lowest possible ISO setting while still achieving a balanced exposure. In bright conditions, start with ISO 100 or 200, while in darker environments, you may need to raise it to ISO 800 or higher. Keep in mind that higher ISO values can introduce noise, so be cautious not to push it too far.

4. Focal Length: A wide-angle lens (e.g., 16-35mm) can help emphasize the grandeur of a spiral staircase or an architectural element, while a longer focal length (e.g., 70-200mm) can compress the scene and draw attention to specific details. Experiment with different focal lengths to find the one that best captures your vision.

5. Focus: Use manual focus or single-point autofocus to ensure the desired portion of the scene is sharp. For staircases, consider focusing on the most prominent or interesting part of the structure, such as the central column or a distinctive railing.

6. White Balance: Set the white balance to match the lighting conditions, or shoot in RAW format to adjust it in post-processing. Daylight or cloudy white balance settings often work well for natural light, while tungsten or fluorescent settings may be more appropriate for artificial light sources.
7. Exposure Compensation: If your camera's metering system isn't producing the desired exposure, use exposure compensation to make adjustments. Increase the value for a brighter image or decrease it for a darker one.

The best settings will depend on the specific scene and your creative intent to capture the perfect shot of your architectural subject.

38. A musical performance or musician

Harmonizing the Lens: Capturing the Magic of Musical Performances and Musicians

Ladies and gentlemen, shutterbugs and music aficionados, gather 'round and let me regale you with the spellbinding world of photographing musical performances and musicians.

It's a visual symphony, where every click of the shutter creates a crescendo of stunning visuals and heart-stirring melodies.

So, put on your dancing shoes, grab your camera, and let's embark on a journey to immortalize the euphonic artistry of the stage!

The Pre-Show Warm-Up:

Before you even set foot in the venue, it's essential to prepare yourself and your gear for the adventure that awaits. As the saying goes, "An ounce of prevention is worth a pound of blurry photos." Well, maybe I just made that up, but it's still true!

Make sure your camera is clean and fully charged, with plenty of memory cards on hand. A tripod might also be a helpful sidekick to stabilize your shots, especially in low-light conditions.

The Stage is Set:

Once you arrive, take a moment to survey the environment. Like a maestro before a performance, you must familiarize yourself with the stage, the lighting, and the possible angles from which to capture the magic.

Don't forget to consider the musicians' movements and how you can best frame their artistic expressions. Remember, every venue is unique, and so too should be your approach to photographing it.

Shutter Speed Symphony:

Now that you've scoped out the scene, it's time to dive into the technical nitty-gritty. The key to capturing a mesmerizing performance is understanding shutter speed. Dance with the music and sync your shutter speed to the rhythm, letting your camera sway and snap with the tempo. Try different settings to create motion blur for a more dynamic feel or freeze the action to capture the intensity of the moment.

Aperture Melodies:

Next on our photographic playlist is aperture. Think of aperture as the conductor of the show, controlling the amount of light that enters your camera. Wide apertures (lower f-stop numbers) will allow more light in, which is particularly useful for indoor or nighttime performances. The side effect? A shallower depth of field, making your subject stand out amidst a beautifully blurred background. It's like having your very own bokeh orchestra!

ISO Serenades:

Last but not least, we have ISO. This setting determines your camera's sensitivity to light, and it's your job to make sure it hits the right note. A higher ISO will be needed in low-light settings, but be careful not to crank it up too high or you'll be left with a noisy, grainy encore.
Find that sweet spot, and your images will be singing the praises of the performance.

Candid Crescendos:

Don't limit yourself to photographing just the performance; the magic of music can be found off-stage as well. Candid shots of musicians tuning their instruments, prepping backstage, or interacting with fans provide a unique glimpse into their world.
These candid moments can be as captivating as the performance itself, allowing you to tell a more comprehensive story of the event.

The Finale:

Photographing musical performances and musicians is a vibrant, exhilarating experience that allows you to fuse the art of photography with the emotional resonance of music. As you venture into this world, remember to let your passion and creativity guide you.
Embrace the rhythm, play with light, and create a visual symphony that will resonate with your audience.

The stage is set, my friends, and it's time to let your lens sing!

Camera Settings

While there's no one-size-fits-all formula for camera settings when photographing musical performances and musicians, here's a general guideline to get you started. Keep in mind that you'll need to adjust these settings based on the specific lighting conditions and your creative vision.

1. Shutter Speed: 1/60 - 1/250 seconds
- Faster shutter speeds (1/125 - 1/250 seconds) will help freeze motion and capture sharper images of fast-moving subjects.
- Slower shutter speeds (1/60 seconds or even slower) can be used to intentionally create motion blur, adding a sense of movement and energy to your photos.

2. Aperture: f/2.8 - f/5.6
- A wide aperture (lower f-stop number, such as f/2.8) allows more light to enter the camera, which is beneficial in low-light situations. This setting also creates a shallow depth of field, drawing focus to your subject while blurring the background.
- If you want a deeper depth of field or are working with more abundant light, you can opt for a narrower aperture (higher f-stop number, such as f/5.6).

3. ISO: 800 - 3200
- For indoor or nighttime performances, you'll likely need a higher ISO (1600 - 3200) to compensate for the limited light available. Keep in mind that using a very high ISO can introduce noise and grain into your images.
- If you're photographing an outdoor daytime performance or the stage is well-lit, you can use a lower ISO (800 or even lower) to maintain a cleaner image with less noise.

4. White Balance: Auto or custom white balance depending on the lighting conditions
- Auto white balance (AWB) can be a safe choice for many situations, but sometimes stage lighting can be challenging for AWB to interpret correctly.
- In these cases, experiment with different white balance presets (such as Tungsten or Fluorescent) or set a custom white balance to achieve accurate color reproduction.

5. Focus Mode: Continuous Autofocus (AF-C) or Single Autofocus (AF-S)
- Continuous Autofocus (AF-C) is suitable for tracking moving subjects, ensuring that they remain in focus throughout the performance.
- Single Autofocus (AF-S) can be used when the subject's movement is minimal or predictable.

Adjust as needed to create the perfect harmony between your camera and the performance.

39. A dancer or other performing artist

Capturing the Rhythm: Photographing Dancers and Performing Artists

There you are, you're standing in the wings of a bustling theater, camera in hand, eagerly waiting for the curtains to part and reveal the vibrant world of performing arts. The music starts, and the stage comes alive with the hypnotic movements of dancers or the emotive expressions of actors. Suddenly, you're transported into their world, a place where reality blurs with fantasy, and your mission becomes clear: to immortalize these fleeting moments of magic through the art of photography.

But where do you begin? Fear not, my friend, for I am here to guide you on this exhilarating journey of capturing the essence of dancers and performing artists.

1. Timing is Everything
As in life, timing in photography is crucial. To catch that perfect pirouette or the apex of a gravity-defying leap, you must develop a keen sense of anticipation. Get to know your subject and their performance.
Study their movements, understand the rhythm of the piece, and be prepared to click the shutter at just the right moment. Remember, the perfect shot is a dance between

you and your subject, and timing is the music that orchestrates it all.

2. Lights, Camera, Action!

Lighting is a photographer's best friend and worst enemy. It can create depth, reveal textures, and set the mood, but it can also be unpredictable, especially when photographing live performances. As a photographer, you must learn to embrace the challenges that lighting presents.

Experiment with different angles and positions to find the most flattering light for your subject. Don't be afraid to venture into the shadows or play with contrasts, for there is beauty to be found in the darkness.

3. Composition: The Art of Balance

Ah, composition, the secret sauce that separates the mundane from the mesmerizing. When photographing dancers or performing artists, consider the elements of design, such as lines, shapes, and space, and how they interact with your subject. Experiment with the rule of thirds, leading lines, and symmetry to create dynamic and visually engaging images. Be bold, be daring, but most importantly, be balanced.

4. Don't Forget the Emotion

What sets a captivating photograph apart from a mere snapshot is the emotion it evokes. When photographing performers, it's essential to capture not only their physical prowess but also the passion and intensity that drive them. Hone in on their facial expressions, the tension in their muscles, and the connection between them and their fellow performers. Remember, you're not just taking a picture; you're telling a story.

5. Gear Up, But Keep It Simple

Yes, we all love our photography gadgets and gizmos, but when it comes to capturing the heat of the moment, less is often more. Choose a camera and lens that you're comfortable with, one that allows you to be mobile and react quickly to the ever-changing stage. A fast prime lens, such as a 50mm or 85mm, is an excellent choice for low-light conditions and capturing intimate details. And let's not forget the trusty monopod, the unsung hero of stability and sharpness in a sea of movement.

Photographing dancers and performing artists is an exciting and rewarding pursuit, one that challenges and inspires both technically and creatively.
So, grab your camera, step into the spotlight, and let the rhythm of the stage guide you in capturing the beauty and emotion of the performing arts.
And remember, when the curtain falls, and the applause fades, it's the images you've created that will keep the magic alive, one frame at a time.

Camera Settings

When it comes to photographing dancers and performing artists, selecting the right camera settings is crucial for capturing sharp, well-exposed images that convey the emotion and movement of the performance. Here's a list of suggested settings to get you started:

1. Shutter Speed: To freeze motion and minimize motion blur, aim for a fast shutter speed, ideally between 1/250 and 1/1000 of a second, depending on the speed of the performer's movements. For more artistic shots, you can experiment with slower shutter speeds to capture motion blur intentionally.

2. Aperture: A wide aperture (low f-number) will allow more light into the camera, which is helpful in low-light conditions typically found in theaters and performance spaces. Additionally, a wide aperture will help create a shallow depth of field, isolating the subject from the background. Consider using an aperture between f/1.8 and f/2.8.

3. ISO: To compensate for low-light environments, you'll need to increase the ISO setting. Be cautious, though, as higher ISO values can introduce digital noise to your images. Depending on your camera's capabilities, an ISO range of 800 to 3200 should be sufficient. Some modern cameras can handle even higher ISO values with minimal noise.

4. Autofocus: Use continuous autofocus (AI Servo for Canon, AF-C for Nikon, and C-AF for other brands) to track the performer's movement and maintain sharp focus. Additionally, select a focus point or area that best corresponds to the subject's position in the frame.

5. Drive Mode: Set your camera to continuous shooting (burst mode) to capture a series of images in rapid succession, increasing the chances of getting the perfect shot.

6. White Balance: Theatrical lighting can be quite varied, so choose a white balance setting that best matches the lighting conditions. Auto white balance (AWB) can be a good starting point, but you may also experiment with custom or preset white balance settings (e.g., Tungsten, Fluorescent) based on the light sources used in the performance.

7. File Format: Shoot in RAW format to preserve the most image data, giving you greater flexibility and control when post-processing your photos. If your camera supports it, you can also shoot in RAW+JPEG mode, which saves both a RAW and a JPEG version of each image.

Trial and error is so often the best way to find the perfect combination that works for you and your subject.

40. A colorful door or window

The Allure of Capturing Colorful Doors and Windows: A Journey Through the Lens

Do you ever find yourself walking through a quaint neighborhood or meandering through a charming village, completely enamored by the vibrant doors and windows that seem to tell a story of their own? Well, you're not alone.
Photographing these captivating subjects has a way of pulling us in, and today, we're going to explore the enchanting world of door and window photography. So, grab your camera and let's dive into this colorful adventure!

The first step in capturing a stunning image of a door or window is to understand the allure of these seemingly mundane objects. The beauty lies in their simplicity – a single door or window can be a portal to an entirely different world.

Colorful doors and windows often hold the key to a home's soul, revealing secrets, emotions, and dreams, all while playing hide-and-seek with the viewer's imagination. It's no wonder we're all so smitten!

Now, let's discuss the art of composition – a photographer's best friend. When you're framing a shot, consider the rule of thirds. This tried-and-true technique involves dividing your frame into nine equal squares and placing the subject along the lines or at the intersections.

It's like tic-tac-toe, but with a splash of color and pizzazz! This will create a balanced and visually appealing photograph, and who wouldn't want that?

As you're seeking out that perfect door or window, don't forget to explore different perspectives. Challenge yourself to find unique angles that will make your viewer's jaw drop. Crouch down low, climb up high, or even tilt your camera for a daring diagonal shot – after all, photography is about pushing boundaries!

Remember, every door has a silver lining, but it's your job to find it and capture it in your frame.

When photographing doors and windows, light is your best ally, and sometimes, your most formidable nemesis. Use natural light to your advantage, as it can create dramatic shadows and stunning contrasts. Play with the sunlight's direction, intensity, and color temperature, and watch as your image transforms before your very eyes.

Golden hour – that magical time just after sunrise or before sunset – is the superhero of light, swooping in to save the day with its warm, gentle glow.

Lastly, let's not forget the power of post-processing. With the help of editing software, you can bring your colorful door or window to life. Adjust the saturation, brightness, and contrast to make the colors pop, or apply filters to create a vintage or dreamy effect. Just remember, with great power comes great responsibility – don't go overboard and lose the essence of your original capture!

In conclusion, photographing colorful doors and windows can be a delightful journey filled with endless possibilities. By understanding the allure, mastering composition, experimenting with perspective, embracing natural light, and polishing your images in post-processing, you'll be well on your way to creating captivating photographs that leave your viewers wanting more.

So, go on – open the door to a world of inspiration and let your creativity flow!

Camera Settings

The "best" camera settings for photographing colorful doors and windows can vary depending on your specific camera model, the available light, and your creative vision. However, here are some general guidelines to help you capture stunning images:

1. ISO: Keep your ISO as low as possible to minimize noise in your images, typically between 100-400.

In low-light conditions or when shooting
handheld, you may need to increase the ISO to
prevent camera shake and maintain sharpness.

2. Aperture: Choose an aperture setting based on
    your desired depth of field. For a sharp, focused
    door or window with a blurred background, use a
    wide aperture (e.g., f/2.8 or f/4). If you want more
    of the scene in focus, opt for a smaller aperture
    (e.g., f/8 or f/11).

3. Shutter Speed: Select a shutter speed that ensures
    a sharp image, especially when shooting handheld.
    As a rule of thumb, use a shutter speed at least as
    fast as the inverse of your focal length (e.g., 1/50th
    of a second for a 50mm lens). Adjust the shutter
    speed accordingly based on the available light and
    your chosen ISO and aperture settings.

4. White Balance: Set the white balance to "Auto" or
    choose a preset that best matches the lighting
    conditions (e.g., "Daylight" for sunny conditions,
    "Shade" for shooting in the shade). You can also
    fine-tune the white balance in post-processing if
    you're shooting in RAW format.

5. Focus Mode: Use Single-shot AF (autofocus) or
    manual focus to ensure your door or window is in
    sharp focus. If your subject has intricate details or
    you want to focus on a specific area, consider using
    the camera's focus points to select your desired
    focus point.

6. Drive Mode: Set your camera to single-shot drive
    mode, as you'll likely be taking one shot at a time
    when photographing doors and windows.

7. Metering Mode: Use Matrix/Evaluative metering
    for an overall balanced exposure. If you find the
    door or window is too dark or bright, you can
    switch to Spot metering and meter off your subject
    directly.
8. Image Format: Shoot in RAW format, if possible,
    to give you more flexibility in post-processing.
    RAW files retain more detail and allow for better
    adjustments in exposure, white balance, and color.

41. A busy airport or train station

Capturing the Energy of Transportation Hubs: An Adventure in Airport and Train Station Photography

The hustle and bustle of a busy airport or train station - it's a photographer's dream! These lively hubs are brimming with emotions and energy, and they offer endless opportunities to create stunning visual narratives.
So, buckle up, my fellow photography enthusiasts, and let's embark on a thrilling journey through the world of transportation photography.

First things first - always be prepared! Before diving into the exciting chaos of an airport or train station, ensure that you have all the essential gear: a trusty camera, a versatile lens (preferably a zoom lens for those dynamic shots), extra batteries, and memory cards. You don't want to miss that once-in-a-lifetime shot because your gear decided to take an unexpected vacation!

Now that you're geared up, it's time to embrace the madness. Take a moment to soak in the atmosphere and feel the energy pulsating through the crowd. There's something almost poetic about the organized chaos of people scurrying to their next destination.

One of the most powerful aspects of transportation photography is capturing the emotion of the moment. From tearful goodbyes to joyful reunions, airports and train stations are packed with poignant stories waiting to be told.

So keep your eyes peeled for those touching moments - the tearful embrace of a soldier returning home, or the wide-eyed excitement of a child seeing a train for the first time. These are the moments that will truly tug at your viewers' heartstrings.

Don't forget to be adventurous with your angles! Get down low for a unique perspective, or climb to higher ground for an expansive bird's-eye view of the bustling terminal. Experiment with depth of field, and play with light and shadows to create a sense of drama. Remember, fortune favors the bold photographer!

But wait, there's more! Airports and train stations are also fantastic locations to practice your street photography skills. From fashionable jet-setters to weary travelers, there's no shortage of interesting subjects. And if you're feeling a bit sneaky, try some candid shots - they're the paparazzi's bread and butter for a reason.

Ah, but we mustn't neglect the architectural beauty of these transportation hubs. Many airports and train stations boast impressive designs, which can make for striking photographic subjects. So, don't hesitate to step back and admire the grandeur of these modern-day cathedrals to travel. After all, it's not all about the people!

Now, my friends, a word of caution: be aware of the rules and regulations at your chosen location. Some airports and train stations may have restrictions on photography, so it's essential to do your research and respect the guidelines. No one wants to be escorted out by security, right? That's a different kind of photo op you'd rather avoid.

So there you have it - your comprehensive guide to the exhilarating world of airport and train station photography. With a keen eye, a sense of adventure, and a dash of creativity, you'll be well on your way to capturing the magic of these bustling transportation hubs.

Remember to stay open to unexpected moments and embrace the organized chaos. And always, always keep your camera at the ready - because you never know when that perfect shot will come speeding your way!

Camera Settings

Camera settings are subjective and depend on various factors such as lighting conditions, your gear, and your creative vision. However, here are some general recommendations to help you capture stunning photos at busy airports and train stations:

1. Aperture: Use a wide aperture (e.g., f/2.8 to f/4) to achieve a shallow depth of field and create an attractive background blur. This helps isolate your subject amidst the bustling environment. For architectural shots or when more depth is desired, opt for a narrower aperture (e.g., f/8 to f/11).

2. Shutter Speed: To freeze fast-moving subjects, use a fast shutter speed (e.g., 1/250s or faster). If you wish to convey motion blur, experiment with slower shutter speeds (e.g., 1/30s or slower). Keep in mind that using a tripod or image stabilization will help avoid camera shake when shooting with slow shutter speeds.

3. ISO: In well-lit areas, keep your ISO low (e.g., ISO 100-200) to minimize noise. In low-light conditions or when shooting handheld with fast shutter speeds, you may need to increase your ISO (e.g., ISO 800-3200). Modern cameras can handle higher ISOs without significant loss of image quality, but it's essential to find a balance that works for your specific camera.

4. White Balance: Set your white balance according to the lighting conditions. In most cases, the "Auto" or "Daylight" settings will work well, but feel free to adjust as needed. If you're shooting in RAW format, you can fine-tune the white balance during post-processing.

5. Autofocus: Use single-point or continuous autofocus, depending on your subject. For static subjects, single-point autofocus is suitable, whereas continuous autofocus is ideal for tracking moving

subjects. Some cameras offer eye or face detection, which can be helpful when capturing people in busy environments.

6. Drive Mode: For capturing fast-paced moments, switch to burst or continuous shooting mode. This allows you to take multiple shots in quick succession, increasing your chances of capturing that perfect moment.

7. Image Format: If possible, shoot in RAW format to preserve the most image data and have greater flexibility during post-processing. If your camera doesn't support RAW or you prefer not to edit your images, opt for the highest quality JPEG setting.

The key is to be adaptable and make the most of the creative possibilities available in your camera... and to expect the unexpected!

42. A public garden or park

A Walk in the Park: Unleashing the Photographer Within

The great outdoors! Who wouldn't love to capture the vibrant hues of a public garden or the serene landscapes of a park? Whether you're a budding photographer or a seasoned pro, there's always something magical about taking your camera on a stroll through nature. Grab your favorite lens, pack a snack, and let's explore the wondrous world of garden and park photography together!

When it comes to photographing a public garden or park, it's all about the art of observation. Take a moment to really drink in the scenery, and you'll soon find that inspiration is as abundant as the petals on a rosebush.
Every corner presents a new opportunity: the play of light and shadows on a wooden bench, the whimsy of a squirrel darting across a path, or the simple elegance of a lone dandelion in a sea of green grass.

Timing is everything in photography, and nature has its own rhythm. Early morning and late afternoon are the prime times to catch that "golden hour" glow, where the warm light can transform even the most ordinary scene into something truly magical. But don't let a cloudy day get you down! Overcast skies can be a blessing in disguise, providing soft, even lighting that's perfect for capturing the subtle details of a dew-kissed flower.

Speaking of flowers, they're the dazzling superstars of any garden or park. To create a captivating floral portrait, get up close and personal with your subject. Use a macro lens or the macro mode on your camera to reveal the intricate beauty of a blossom's petals, or experiment with depth of field to make your subject pop against a dreamy, blurred background. Remember, in the world of photography, it's okay to stop and smell the roses—as long as you capture them in all their glory!

Now, let's talk about the unsung heroes of park photography: trees. These majestic giants offer a wealth of opportunities for creative compositions. Look for interesting textures in the bark, or use the intricate patterns of branches to create natural frames for your subjects. When autumn rolls around, get ready to have a field day with the explosion of color that will have you leaf-peeping through your viewfinder.

Don't forget that gardens and parks are more than just flora and fauna—they're also a stage for human stories to unfold. Keep an eye out for tender moments between couples, the infectious laughter of a group of friends, or the quiet contemplation of a solitary visitor. These candid snapshots can breathe life and emotion into your garden and park photography, turning them into visual narratives that resonate with viewers.

And while you're busy capturing the beauty around you, don't be afraid to break the "rules" every now and then. Try unconventional angles, play with exposure, or experiment with different lenses. After all, rules are meant to be broken, right? Just like the rule about not stepping on the grass (but please, do respect the park rules).

Photographing a public garden or park is a delightful and rewarding experience that allows you to connect with the natural world while honing your photography skills. So, get out there, explore, and let your creativity bloom like a sunflower on a sunny day.

Remember, the best camera is the one you have with you, so make every shot count and fill your memory card with unforgettable moments. And who knows? You might just find that your next masterpiece is waiting for you right around the corner, nestled between the petals of a daisy or under the shade of a mighty oak.

Camera Settings

When it comes to capturing the beauty of public gardens and parks, there's no one-size-fits-all approach to camera settings. However, here are some suggestions to help you get started on your photographic journey:

1. Aperture: Use a wide aperture (low f-number) like f/1.8 or f/2.8 for shallow depth of field, isolating your subject and creating a beautiful, blurred

background (bokeh). For landscape shots or group photos, use a smaller aperture (higher f-number) like f/8 or f/11 to keep more of the scene in focus.

2. Shutter Speed: Choose a fast shutter speed (e.g., 1/500 or faster) to freeze movement when capturing wildlife, playing children, or water features. For static subjects or scenes, you can opt for a slower shutter speed (e.g., 1/60 or 1/125) depending on the available light.

3. ISO: Aim for the lowest possible ISO setting (e.g., ISO 100 or 200) to minimize noise and achieve the best image quality. Increase the ISO when shooting in low-light conditions, but keep in mind that higher ISO values may introduce more noise into your images.

4. White Balance: Set the white balance according to the lighting conditions (e.g., sunny, cloudy, or shade) to ensure accurate colors. Alternatively, use the auto white balance (AWB) function and fine-tune the colors later during post-processing.

5. Focus Mode: For stationary subjects, use single-shot autofocus (AF-S or One-Shot AF). For moving subjects or unpredictable situations, switch to continuous autofocus (AF-C or AI Servo AF) to track the subject and maintain focus.

6. Metering Mode: Use matrix or evaluative metering for even lighting conditions or when the subject is well-lit. Switch to spot metering for high-contrast scenes or when you want to expose for a specific part of the image.

7. Drive Mode: Choose single-shot mode for most situations, but switch to continuous or burst mode when capturing fast-moving subjects or fleeting moments.

The key to mastering garden and park photography is to try different settings and techniques, and most importantly, to enjoy the process!

43. A person engaged in their hobby or craft

Capturing the Essence: The Art of Photographing Hobbyists and Crafters

I'm sure we've all seen the delicate hands of a potter skillfully shaping a lump of clay into an exquisite vase, or a woodworker's chisel carving intricate patterns into a piece of timber. These moments are fleeting, yet they carry immense power and emotion.

As a photography enthusiast, it's your mission to encapsulate these magical instances in your frame, and today, we're going to explore the art of photographing people engaged in their hobbies or crafts.

Before we delve into the details, let's pause for a moment to appreciate the beauty of our subjects. Hobbyists and crafters are passionate souls, pouring their hearts and skills into their crafts. They radiate a unique energy that translates effortlessly into evocative images. With that in mind, let's dive into the world of capturing the essence of these creators.

1. Connect with your subject To truly capture the spirit of your subject, establish a connection with them. Engage in conversation, learn about their passion, and share your own photography zeal. The more comfortable they are with you, the more genuine

and captivating your images will be. Remember, a picture is worth a thousand words, but a meaningful connection can elevate that to a million!

2. Embrace the environment Crafters and hobbyists often work in spaces filled with character, from cluttered workshops to cozy art studios. Embrace the environment, and let it tell the story. Capture the paint-splattered easel, the wood shavings on the floor, or the array of fabric swatches in a seamstress's sewing room. These details add context and depth to your images, making them even more captivating.

3. Focus on the details When photographing someone at work, it's essential to get up close and personal. Focus on the details that reveal their process and passion. Think of the paintbrush gliding across a canvas, the knitter's fingers deftly maneuvering yarn, or the baker's hands kneading dough. By honing in on these actions, you'll create a visual narrative that captures the essence of their craft.

4. Experiment with angles and perspectives To keep things interesting, play around with different angles and perspectives. Photograph your subject from above as they work, or try a worm's-eye view to emphasize their mastery. Be bold, be creative, and don't be afraid to think outside the (camera) box.

5. Capture the emotion Crafting and hobbies are emotional outlets, and as a photographer, your job is to translate that emotion into your images. Be on the lookout for the joy in a dancer's leap, the concentration etched on a painter's face, or the

satisfaction of a gardener tending to their plants. By capturing these emotions, you'll create a visual symphony that resonates with your audience.

6. Play with light and shadow Lighting is a photographer's best friend, and when it comes to photographing hobbyists, it can add a whole new dimension to your images. Experiment with natural light streaming through windows, or play with shadows cast by tools and equipment. By manipulating light and shadow, you'll add depth and drama to your compositions.

7. Don't forget the candid moments While posed portraits have their place, the true magic lies in candid moments. Keep your camera at the ready, and be prepared to capture the unexpected. These spontaneous snapshots will immortalize the raw essence of your subject and their passion.

Photographing people engaged in their hobbies or crafts is an art form in itself. By connecting with your subject, embracing their environment, focusing on details, experimenting with angles, capturing emotion, playing with light, and seizing candid moments, you'll create images that tell a compelling

Camera Settings

While there's no one-size-fits-all solution for camera settings, here's a general guide to help you achieve stunning results when photographing hobbyists and crafters. Keep in mind that these settings may vary based on your camera, the environment, and your creative vision.

1. Aperture: Use a wide aperture (low f-number) like f/1.8 or f/2.8 to create a shallow depth of field. This will help isolate your subject from the background, drawing attention to the person and their craft. If you want more of the environment in focus, opt for a narrower aperture (higher f-number) like f/8 or f/11.

2. Shutter Speed: For capturing sharp, detailed images of people at work, use a fast shutter speed, such as 1/125th or 1/250th of a second. If the subject's movements are quicker or if you're aiming for a motion blur effect, adjust the shutter speed accordingly (e.g., 1/500th or 1/1000th of a second).

3. ISO: Keep the ISO as low as possible, ideally around 100-400, to minimize noise and preserve image quality. If you're shooting in a low-light environment or want to use a faster shutter speed, you may need to increase the ISO. Just remember that higher ISO values may result in grainier images.

4. White Balance: Set your white balance to "Auto" or choose an appropriate preset for the lighting conditions (e.g., "Daylight" for natural light or "Tungsten" for incandescent bulbs). Alternatively, you can use the custom white balance feature to ensure accurate colors.

5. Focus Mode: Use single-point autofocus (AF-S for Nikon or One-Shot AF for Canon) to ensure precise

focus on your subject. For moving subjects or continuous action, switch to continuous autofocus (AF-C for Nikon or AI Servo AF for Canon).

6. Drive Mode: Set your camera to single-shot mode for deliberate, composed images. If you want to capture a series of rapid-fire shots to freeze action or catch a fleeting moment, switch to continuous shooting mode (also known as burst mode).

7. Metering Mode: Use matrix or evaluative metering for balanced exposure across the entire frame. If your subject is backlit or in a high-contrast environment, consider using spot metering to ensure proper exposure for the person and their craft.

44. A neon sign or other interesting light source

It's A Kind of Neon Magic!

Have you ever walked down a bustling city street at night, mesmerized by the vibrant glow of neon signs that seem to dance before your eyes? If so, buckle up, because we're about to embark on a dazzling adventure into the world of neon sign photography!
Neon signs and intriguing light sources are like electrifying treasures, waiting to be discovered and captured by your trusty camera. With a touch of creativity and a splash of enthusiasm, you'll soon be able to transform these luminous gems into stunning, Insta-worthy masterpieces.

Step 1: Find Your Neon Nirvana
The first step to capturing the neon sign of your dreams is - you guessed it - finding it! You'll want to scout out locations with a concentration of neon signs or intriguing light sources. Think city centers, entertainment districts, or even that funky little bar around the corner. Remember, the more unique the sign, the more captivating your photo will be.

Step 2: Timing is Everything
While neon signs can look fabulous any time of day, they truly come to life after dusk. The contrast between the radiant neon colors and the velvety darkness of the night

sky is pure photographic poetry. So grab your camera and venture out into the twilight – just don't forget your jacket, it gets nippy out there!

Step 3: Set Your Camera Up for Success

When photographing neon signs or other vibrant light sources, it's crucial to adjust your camera settings to achieve the desired effect. Keep your ISO low (100-400) to avoid noise, and use a smaller aperture (f/8-f/11) for a sharp image. Your shutter speed will depend on the ambient light, so feel free to experiment. And if your camera has a "night mode" or "low light mode," give it a whirl!

Step 4: Stabilize Yourself (and Your Camera)

Let's face it, even the steadiest of hands can turn into a wobbly mess when trying to capture a long exposure shot. That's where tripods come in! A sturdy tripod will ensure your camera stays still during those critical seconds, giving you a crisp, clear image. No tripod, no problem! Improvise with a nearby ledge, table, or even a pile of books (just make sure it's stable!).

Step 5: Play with Perspectives

When it comes to neon sign photography, the only limit is your imagination. Get up close and personal with your subject, or take a step back to capture the entire scene. Try shooting from different angles, like a low-angle shot to emphasize the size of the sign or a high-angle shot for a bird's-eye view. You could even use a wide-angle lens or create a panorama to capture an entire street of glowing signs!

Step 6: Go Forth and Edit

Post-processing is where the real magic happens. With a few simple tweaks in your favorite photo editing software, you can enhance colors, adjust exposure, and add filters to create a true work of art. Just don't go too overboard with the adjustments – remember, less is more!

And there you have it, a vibrant journey through the world of neon sign photography. So grab your camera, hit the streets, and unleash your inner shutterbug – the neon jungle awaits! And remember, in the wise words of Ansel Adams, "You don't take a photograph, you make it." Now, go make some neon magic!

Camera Settings

To capture the enchanting beauty of neon signs or captivating light sources, consider the following camera settings as a starting point:

1. Mode: Manual (M) or Aperture Priority (A/Av) mode to have full control over your camera settings.
2. ISO: Keep the ISO low, around 100-400, to minimize noise and maintain image quality. If your scene is particularly dark, you might need to

increase the ISO, but be cautious about introducing too much noise.

3. Aperture: Use a smaller aperture, such as f/8 to f/11, to achieve a sharp image with a greater depth of field. This will help keep both the neon sign and its surroundings in focus.

4. Shutter Speed: Start with a shutter speed of around 1/60 or 1/125, and adjust based on the ambient light and desired effect. If you want to capture light trails or motion blur, use a slower shutter speed. Always ensure that your shutter speed is fast enough to avoid camera shake or use a tripod to stabilize your shot.

5. White Balance: Set your white balance to "Auto" or choose a specific setting based on the lighting conditions, such as "Tungsten" or "Fluorescent" if you're photographing under artificial lights.

6. Focus Mode: Choose "Single-Servo Autofocus" (AF-S) or "One-Shot AF" mode to lock focus on your subject, ensuring a sharp image.

7. Metering Mode: Use "Spot Metering" or "Center-Weighted Metering" to expose your image correctly based on the brightness of the neon sign.

8. Image Format: Shoot in RAW format to capture the highest level of detail and have more flexibility during post-processing.

Happy neon hunting!

45. A vintage car or mode of transportation

Rolling Back Time: Capturing Vintage Cars and Classic Modes of Transportation

For a lot of people, there is a real allure to vintage cars and classic modes of transportation! They evoke memories of bygone eras, the sound of their engines purring like a contented cat, and the smell of history that surrounds them.

If you're anything like me, you're itching to capture these masterpieces of engineering through the lens of your camera. So buckle up, dear reader, as we embark on a photographic journey to do justice to these magnificent time machines.

First and foremost, let's talk about the location. While a dusty garage may house these beauties, it won't do them any favors in your photographs. Take your subject out for a spin and find a fitting backdrop to complement its charm.

Consider historic sites, rustic barns, or even a picturesque countryside road. A well-chosen location not only adds context to your shot but also gives your viewers a sense of time travel—vroom, vroom!

Lighting is, of course, key in any genre of photography, and capturing vintage transportation is no exception. The soft, warm light of the golden hour (shortly after sunrise or before sunset) casts an enchanting glow on your subject, accentuating its curves and enhancing its color.
If you're feeling adventurous, you might even experiment with a little moonlight photography—nothing says "romantic" like an antique car bathed in the silvery light of the moon.

Don't be afraid to get up close and personal with your subject. Details make all the difference when photographing vintage cars and other modes of transportation.
Capture the intricate craftsmanship of the dashboard, the retro upholstery, and the gleaming chrome accents. These little details tell a story of their own, and trust me, they'll make your photographs stand out like a classic Cadillac in a sea of modern compacts.

Angles, my dear photographer, are your best friend. Experiment with different perspectives to add depth and interest to your shots. Get down low and shoot from the ground up, or climb a nearby hill for a bird's eye view. Capture the car head-on for a powerful, imposing shot or from the rear for a touch of mystery. Remember, there's no "one size fits all" approach, so don't be shy about exploring new angles. The more, the merrier!

Now, let's talk about the human element. While these classic vehicles are stunning on their own, adding people to your photographs can breathe life into your images. Invite the owner, dressed in period attire, to pose with their prized possession. Or, arrange a vintage-themed picnic, complete with a wicker basket and checkered blanket, to create a nostalgic scene.

The possibilities are endless, so channel your inner director and create a visual story that transports your viewers to a different era.

Finally, post-processing is the cherry on top of your photographic sundae. Enhance your images with subtle adjustments, such as boosting the saturation of your colors, adding a soft vignette, or applying a vintage film preset.

Remember, less is more, so strive for a natural look that complements the subject, rather than overpowering it.
In conclusion, photographing vintage cars and classic modes of transportation is a delightful and rewarding pursuit.

Keep these tips in mind, and you'll soon be creating timeless images that celebrate the beauty and charm of these historical treasures. So, dust off your camera, rev up your creative engine, and let's hit the road for some awe-inspiring photographic adventures!

Camera Settings

While specific camera settings will vary depending on the lighting conditions and your creative vision, here are some general guidelines to help you capture stunning images of vintage cars and classic modes of transportation:

1. Aperture: Use a wide aperture (low f-number, e.g., f/2.8 to f/5.6) to create a shallow depth of field, isolating your subject and creating a beautiful background blur (bokeh). For capturing intricate details or group scenes, opt for a smaller aperture (higher f-number, e.g., f/8 to f/11) to ensure a greater depth of field.

2. Shutter Speed: Aim for a shutter speed that's fast enough to freeze any motion and eliminate camera shake. A good starting point is 1/125th of a second or faster. If you're using a tripod or shooting stationary subjects, you can experiment with slower shutter speeds.

3. ISO: Keep your ISO setting as low as possible (e.g., ISO 100 or 200) to minimize noise and maintain image quality. In low light situations, you may need to increase your ISO (e.g., ISO 800 or higher), but be mindful of the trade-off between higher sensitivity and increased noise.

4. White Balance: Set your white balance to "Auto" or choose a preset that matches the lighting conditions

(e.g., "Daylight" for sunny days, "Shade" for overcast conditions, or "Tungsten" for incandescent lighting). You can also experiment with custom white balance settings to achieve a specific mood or color cast.

5. Focus Mode: Use single-shot autofocus (AF-S or One-Shot AF) for stationary subjects and continuous autofocus (AF-C or AI Servo AF) if you're capturing moving subjects or working with unpredictable elements, such as wind-blown leaves or passing pedestrians.

6. Drive Mode: Set your camera to single-shot mode for posed, static scenes or continuous shooting (burst) mode if you're capturing action or rapidly changing expressions and poses.

7. File Format: Shoot in RAW format to retain maximum image data, allowing for greater flexibility during post-processing. If your camera doesn't support RAW or you prefer minimal editing, use the highest quality JPEG setting.

8. Metering Mode: Choose a metering mode that best suits the scene's lighting conditions. Evaluative or matrix metering works well for evenly lit scenes, while spot metering is ideal for high-contrast situations or when you need to meter off a specific area of the frame.

46. A foggy or misty scene

The Enchanting Allure of Foggy Photography: Capturing the Ethereal Magic

Imagine yourself waking up early on a chilly morning, stepping outside, and being greeted by a mesmerizing blanket of fog or mist. The world around you seems transformed, mysterious, and full of enchanting beauty. It's as if nature is inviting you to take out your camera and capture its breathtaking secrets.

Well, my friends, it's time to heed that call and explore the captivating world of foggy and misty photography!

Fog and mist have a unique ability to evoke emotions, create a sense of depth, and add a touch of mystique to your images. These ephemeral scenes, with their fleeting beauty, often make photographers feel as though they've stepped into a dream. But how do you capture this transient wonder?

Fear not, fellow photography enthusiasts, for we shall embark on a journey to unravel the secrets of capturing foggy and misty scenes!

1. Timing is everything: Early bird gets the fog!
While the mysterious world of fog and mist may feel like it's available only to the lucky few, the truth is that timing

is key. Most fog and mist occur in the early morning or late evening when the air is cooler. Set your alarm, grab a hot beverage, and prepare to witness the enchanting transformation of the landscape.

2. Play with exposure: Dance with the light!

Foggy and misty scenes can be tricky when it comes to exposure. Overexposure might cause you to lose the ethereal quality of the fog, while underexposure can result in a dark, uninviting image. To avoid these pitfalls, experiment with your camera's exposure settings or use exposure bracketing. And remember, there's no shame in a little post-processing magic to enhance your foggy masterpiece!

3. Embrace silhouettes: Striking contrasts that beguile!

Silhouettes can be powerful compositional elements in foggy and misty scenes. When backlit by the sun or other light sources, objects shrouded in fog can create striking and mysterious shapes. So go on, let those trees, buildings, or people play hide-and-seek with the fog, and you'll be rewarded with stunning images that leave viewers wanting more.

4. Get up close and personal: A world within a world!

Don't shy away from getting up close to your subjects in foggy conditions. Macro shots of dewdrops on a spider web or mist-laden leaves can reveal the stunning intricacies of nature's tiny wonders. Remember, sometimes the most magnificent secrets lie in the smallest details.

5. Experiment with black and white: Timeless classics!

Black and white photography can work wonders for foggy and misty scenes, emphasizing the contrasts and textures in your images. Stripping away the colors might just reveal the soul of the scene, turning your photographs into timeless masterpieces that evoke a sense of nostalgia and wonder.

Embrace the unknown and let the enchanting world of fog and mist take you on a magical journey. And who knows? You might just find that the fog lifts not only from the landscape but also from the depths of your creative soul.

Now go forth, fellow photographers, and capture the ephemeral beauty of foggy and misty scenes. May your lens be ever ready, and your spirit ever adventurous!

Camera Settings

Capturing the ethereal beauty of foggy and misty scenes requires a fine-tuning of your camera settings. While every situation is unique, here are some general guidelines to help you achieve the best results:

1. Aperture: Opt for a mid-range aperture, such as f/8 to f/11, to achieve a good balance between depth of

field and sharpness. If you're aiming for a shallow depth of field, a wider aperture like f/2.8 to f/5.6 may be more suitable.

2. Shutter Speed: Adjust your shutter speed depending on the amount of light and your desired effect. For example, if you're photographing a foggy landscape with little movement, a slower shutter speed (e.g., 1/30s to 1/60s) might suffice. For fast-moving subjects or to freeze droplets in the air, a faster shutter speed (e.g., 1/250s or higher) may be necessary.

3. ISO: Keep your ISO as low as possible (e.g., 100 or 200) to minimize noise in your images. In darker situations or when using faster shutter speeds, you may need to increase the ISO accordingly. Be mindful of the trade-off between higher ISO settings and increased noise.

4. White Balance: Adjust your white balance to capture the mood and atmosphere of the scene. For foggy or misty conditions, you might want to set your white balance to "cloudy" or "shade" to create a warmer, more inviting feel. Alternatively, you can shoot in RAW format and fine-tune the white balance in post-processing.

5. Focus: Use manual focus if your camera struggles to lock onto subjects in low-contrast foggy scenes. When using autofocus, select a single focus point and aim it at an area of contrast (e.g., the edge of a tree or a person's outline) to ensure accurate focusing.

6. Exposure Compensation: Adjust exposure compensation as needed to avoid overexposed or underexposed images. Start with a neutral setting (e.g., 0 EV) and review your images, making adjustments as required. In foggy conditions, you may need to slightly underexpose (e.g., -1/3 to -2/3 EV) to preserve the atmosphere and depth of the scene.

7. Bracketing: Use exposure bracketing to capture a range of exposures for the same scene. This will give you more flexibility in post-processing and help ensure that you have at least one well-exposed image to work with.

47. An interesting pattern or texture

Capturing the Beauty of Patterns and Textures: A Visual Symphony for the Soul

Photography! The magical art of freezing time, capturing the beauty of the world around us, and painting with light – all at the press of a button. In a world teeming with fascinating patterns and textures, what could be more delightful than capturing these visual delights and creating visual symphonies for our souls?

Today, we'll embark on a journey to explore the incredible world of photographing patterns and textures, and in the process, perhaps you'll fall even more in love with this wonderful art form. Are you ready? Let's dive in!

First things first, let's take a moment to appreciate the sheer abundance of patterns and textures that surround us. From the intricate weave of a spider's web to the mesmerizing swirls in a cup of latte, the world is a veritable treasure trove of eye candy. And the best part? You don't need a fancy camera or exotic location to capture these gems. Sometimes, all it takes is a keen eye and a bit of imagination. So, don your photographer's hat, and let's embark on this visual adventure!

When photographing patterns and textures, the first rule is to embrace your inner Sherlock Holmes. Keep an eye out for details – the world is your oyster, and you're on a quest for visual pearls.

Pay attention to lines, shapes, and colors, and experiment with different angles and perspectives to create unique, eye-catching images. Remember, great photography is all about finding the extraordinary in the ordinary – and who said the ordinary can't be extraordinary?

One of the most important elements of capturing patterns and textures is lighting. Like a master painter, you need to learn how to use light to your advantage to bring out the best in your subject. Try to use natural light whenever possible, as it tends to produce the most pleasing results.

Play with shadows, highlights, and contrast to emphasize the details and create a sense of depth in your images. After all, photography is all about painting with light, and you, my friend, are the artist!

Composition is another essential aspect of photographing patterns and textures. Fill the frame with your subject, and don't be afraid to get up close and personal – sometimes, the most interesting details are hiding in plain sight, just waiting for you to discover them.

Use the rule of thirds, leading lines, and other compositional techniques to create images that are both visually balanced and engaging. Remember, you're the conductor of this visual symphony, and it's up to you to orchestrate a captivating performance!

Finally, don't forget to have fun and let your creativity run wild. Experiment with different camera settings, try out new post-processing techniques, and break the rules – sometimes, the most memorable images are the ones that defy convention.

And if you're ever feeling stuck, just remember the wise words of famed photographer Henri Cartier-Bresson: "Your first 10,000 photographs are your worst." So, keep snapping away, and soon enough, you'll be creating visual masterpieces that capture the beauty and wonder of the world's patterns and textures.

So explore the world through your lens, uncovering the hidden beauty of patterns and textures. Let your imagination soar, and don't forget to enjoy the journey – after all, isn't that what photography is all about?

Camera Settings

The ideal camera settings for photographing patterns and textures will depend on various factors, including lighting conditions, the subject, and your creative vision. However, here's a list of general settings and tips to help you capture stunning images of patterns and textures:

1. Aperture: Opt for a smaller aperture (higher f-number) like f/8 or f/11 to ensure a greater depth of

field, keeping the entire pattern or texture in focus. If you want to isolate a specific part of the pattern or texture, use a wider aperture (lower f-number) to create a shallow depth of field.

2. Shutter Speed: Choose a shutter speed that will produce a sharp image while hand-holding your camera or using a tripod. For handheld shots, a good rule of thumb is to use a shutter speed that is at least the reciprocal of the focal length (e.g., 1/50 for a 50mm lens). In low light situations or when using a tripod, slower shutter speeds may be necessary to capture enough light.

3. ISO: Keep your ISO as low as possible (e.g., 100 or 200) to minimize noise and maintain image quality. Increase the ISO only when necessary, such as in low light conditions or when using faster shutter speeds to freeze motion.

4. Focus: Use manual focus or single-point autofocus to ensure precise focusing on the desired part of the pattern or texture. If your camera offers focus peaking, this can be a helpful tool for nailing the focus in your images.

5. White Balance: Set your white balance to match the lighting conditions, or use auto white balance if you're unsure. You can always fine-tune the white balance during post-processing if shooting in RAW format.

6. Metering: Choose a metering mode that best suits your scene. For most pattern and texture photography, matrix or evaluative metering will provide a balanced exposure. However, if your

subject has high contrast, you might consider using spot metering to expose for the most important part of the image.

7. Shooting Mode: Consider using Aperture Priority mode (A or Av) to maintain control over the depth of field while allowing the camera to set the appropriate shutter speed. If you prefer more control, Manual mode (M) lets you adjust both aperture and shutter speed independently.

8. Image Format: Shoot in RAW format to capture the highest level of detail and have more flexibility during post-processing.

48. A time-lapse of a busy area

A Time-Lapse Tale of a Bustling Cityscape

Have you ever stood amidst the hustle and bustle of a city, feeling the energy pulsating around you, and thought, "I wish I could capture this moment"? Well, fear not, fellow photo enthusiasts!
With the magic of time-lapse photography, you can seize the heart and soul of a busy urban jungle, frame by frame.

Time-lapse photography is like a secret key that unlocks the wonder of life's fleeting moments. Imagine compressing the chaos of a day's worth of bustling commuters, speeding cars, and swirling clouds into a mere minute or two!
With a sprinkle of patience, a dollop of creativity, and a healthy serving of dedication, you can create an awe-inspiring visual symphony.
Ready to dive in? Let's get started on our journey into the vibrant world of time-lapse photography!

Step 1: Scouting the Perfect Location Like a lion on the hunt, a time-lapse photographer must stalk their prey: the perfect vantage point. Wander through your city, absorb the atmosphere, and seek out spots with a rich tapestry of movement. Elevated viewpoints, such as rooftops or bridges, often provide the best perspective. Remember, a bird's-eye view can make even the busiest city look like a game of Tetris on fast-forward!

Step 2: The Gear Game You don't need the latest, greatest, or shiniest gear to capture a stunning time-lapse, but some essentials are non-negotiable. A sturdy tripod, a reliable camera with manual settings, and an intervalometer (a fancy word for a timer) are your trusty companions. Oh, and don't forget a fully charged battery and ample memory card space—after all, Rome wasn't built in a day, and neither is a time-lapse!

Step 3: Timing is Everything Patience, young grasshopper! A truly breathtaking time-lapse takes time—sometimes hours. Decide on the duration of your final video, then calculate how many photos you'll need. For example, if you want a 30-second video with a 24 frames-per-second (fps) playback rate, you'll need 720 photos (30 seconds x 24 fps). With an interval of 5 seconds between shots, it'll take you an hour to capture the full sequence. Got your calculator ready? Great! Let's move on.

Step 4: Setting the Stage Camera settings can make or break your time-lapse masterpiece. Start by selecting manual mode to maintain consistent exposure. Choose a low ISO to avoid digital noise, and opt for a smaller aperture (larger f-number) for a greater depth of field. For shutter speed, try a slower setting to capture the fluid motion of your bustling scene. Of course, there's no one-size-fits-all recipe—experimentation is the spice of life!

Step 5: The Waiting Game With your camera set up and ready to roll, now comes the hardest part: waiting. Channel your inner zen, and let the world unfurl before your lens. Watch as the sun casts its golden glow on the concrete jungle, or as the neon lights of nightlife flicker to life. You might find yourself awestruck by the beauty of the world in motion.

Step 6: Editing Extravaganza Once you've captured your time-lapse sequence, it's time to polish it to perfection in post-production. Combine your images into a video using editing software, then adjust exposure, color balance, and contrast as needed. Add some snazzy music, and voilà! You've created a visual symphony that sings the song of a city on the move.

So there you have it! A step-by-step guide to immortalizing the vibrant pulse of a bustling metropolis in a captivating time-lapse. With a little practice, patience, and a dash of creativity, you'll soon be weaving together stunning visual stories that showcase the dynamic essence of urban life.

And remember, whether you're a seasoned pro or a wide-eyed beginner, the journey of time-lapse photography is an adventure in itself. Embrace the unexpected and revel in the magic of the world unfolding before your eyes. You might even find yourself chuckling at the ant-like frenzy of humanity from your bird's-eye perch.

So scout that perfect location, and get ready to embark on a whirlwind adventure through time and space. The city awaits, and it's your time to capture its ceaseless dance, frame by mesmerizing frame. Now go forth and conquer the time-lapse universe, one click at a time!

Camera Settings

While the ideal camera settings for a time-lapse in a busy area may vary depending on your specific camera model, location, and lighting conditions, here's a general guide to help you get started:

1. Camera Mode: Manual (M) mode – This ensures you have full control over your settings and maintain consistent exposure throughout the time-lapse.
2. ISO: Low (100-200) – A low ISO setting helps minimize digital noise in your images. In low-light situations, you may need to increase the ISO, but try to keep it as low as possible for the best results.
3. Aperture: Small (f/8 to f/16) – A smaller aperture (represented by a larger f-number) results in a greater depth of field, ensuring more of your scene remains in focus.
4. Shutter Speed: Slow (1/4 to 1/30) – A slower shutter speed captures the fluid motion of people and vehicles in a busy area. Experiment to find the ideal speed for the desired motion blur effect.

5. White Balance: Adjust according to lighting conditions or set it to Auto – Proper white balance ensures accurate colors in your time-lapse. If you're shooting during the golden hour or blue hour, you may need to adjust the white balance to capture the warm or cool tones accurately. Alternatively, you can shoot in RAW format and adjust the white balance during post-processing.
6. Image Quality: RAW – Shooting in RAW format captures more image data and provides greater flexibility for editing in post-production.
7. Focus: Manual – Set your focus manually to ensure it remains constant throughout the time-lapse sequence.
8. Interval: 2 to 5 seconds – The interval between each shot depends on the length of your final video and the desired playback rate (fps). A shorter interval will result in a smoother time-lapse, while a longer interval will create a more dramatic effect.

49. A romantic scene

Capturing the Essence of Love: A Guide to Photographing Romantic Scenes

Love is in the air, and so is the sweet aroma of passion, longing, and desire. When it comes to immortalizing these enchanting emotions, photography stands as the perfect medium. But fret not, for this photographic journey need not be a tumultuous affair. With a little guidance, we'll have you snapping romantic masterpieces in no time!

First things first, let's set the stage for love. Choose a location that oozes romance – think intimate cafes, enchanting gardens, or a cozy nook by the fireplace. The key is to find a setting that whispers sweet nothings to the viewer, drawing them in with an irresistible allure.

Next, let's talk about lighting. The magic hour, that ethereal time just before sunset or after sunrise, casts a warm, golden glow perfect for capturing hearts aflutter. Shadows and highlights play a delicate dance during these times, sculpting your subjects and infusing your images with a touch of dreaminess.
But don't be disheartened if the sun isn't on your side; soft, diffused light can be equally enchanting. Play with candles, fairy lights, or even the soft glow from a window to create an intimate atmosphere.

Now, let's get up close and personal with composition. The rule of thirds might be your trusty companion on most photographic adventures, but when it comes to love, feel free to break the rules.

Embrace asymmetry, juxtapose your subjects, and experiment with angles to create dynamic and engaging images. Remember, the heart wants what the heart wants, and sometimes that means taking the road less traveled!

The language of love may be universal, but it can be spoken in many different ways. To truly capture the essence of romance, it's essential to tap into your subjects' unique connection. Encourage your lovebirds to interact – holding hands, stealing glances, or sharing a tender embrace. The more natural and candid these moments are, the more they will resonate with the viewer.

In this world of photographic romance, the details make all the difference. Look for those little moments that reveal the depth of your subjects' bond – an intertwined hand, a soft touch, or a lingering gaze. These are the visual breadcrumbs that lead the viewer down the path of love and passion.

And finally, a word on editing. In post-processing, keep things light and airy. Enhance those warm tones, lift the shadows, and play with curves to accentuate the emotions you've captured. Just remember, less is more; the goal is to enhance the feeling of love, not overshadow it.

So, there you have it – your roadmap to photographing love in all its splendor. As you embark on this journey, remember that true romance lies in the subtle moments and tender connections. And while love may be a many-splendored thing, capturing it in a photograph will leave a lasting impression that transcends the boundaries of time. Now, my dear Cupid, spread your wings and let your camera be your bow and arrow, capturing hearts and souls one click at a time.

Camera Settings

The ideal camera settings for capturing a romantic scene will vary depending on the specific conditions you're shooting in, such as available light and your subjects' movements. However, here's a general guide to get you started:

1. Aperture: To achieve a dreamy, romantic effect, use a wide aperture (low f-number) like f/1.8 or f/2.8. This will create a shallow depth of field, blurring the background and allowing your subjects to stand out. Additionally, a wide aperture lets in more light, which can be helpful in low-light situations.
2. Shutter Speed: Choose a shutter speed that complements the scene. If your subjects are relatively still, a shutter speed around 1/60 to 1/125 should suffice. However, if they're moving or interacting more dynamically, you may need a

faster shutter speed like 1/250 or even 1/500 to freeze the motion and prevent blur.

3. ISO: Keep your ISO as low as possible to maintain image quality and minimize noise. Start with an ISO of 100 or 200, and only increase it if necessary to achieve proper exposure. In low-light situations, you might need to bump up the ISO to 800 or even 1600, but be cautious of excessive noise.

4. White Balance: To capture the warmth and ambiance of a romantic scene, consider setting your white balance to "Shade" or "Cloudy." This will enhance the warm tones in the image. Alternatively, you can shoot in RAW format and adjust the white balance during post-processing for precise control.

5. Focus: Use single-point autofocus (AF) and place the focus point on your subjects' eyes or another key area, ensuring they remain sharp and in focus. You can also experiment with manual focus to achieve a more artistic, soft-focus look if desired.

6. Drive Mode: Switch to continuous shooting mode if you're capturing candid moments or interactions between your subjects. This will allow you to rapidly take multiple shots, increasing the likelihood of capturing that perfect, fleeting moment.

7. Metering Mode: Use spot or center-weighted metering to prioritize exposure for your subjects and ensure their skin tones are accurately captured.

Play with different settings and combinations to discover the perfect recipe for capturing the essence of romance in your photographs.

50. An abandoned building or urban exploration

Urban Exploration: Breathing Life into Abandoned Spaces Through the Lens

Picture yourself standing in front of an abandoned building. The walls whisper stories of the past, and the decaying structure ignites your imagination. You raise your camera and capture the soul of the forgotten space.

Congratulations, my adventurous friend, you've entered the enthralling world of urban exploration photography! Urban exploration, or "urbex" for the cool kids, is the art of exploring and photographing man-made structures that have been abandoned or are usually off-limits.
The pursuit of these relics is a thrilling adventure, and one that allows you to immortalize these silent witnesses of time in your photographs.

Let's dive into the captivating world of urban exploration photography and discover how to breathe life into abandoned spaces through the lens.

Safety First, or How to Make Sure Your Urbex Adventure Doesn't Turn into a Horror Movie

Before you start snapping away at rusty pipes and peeling paint, it's essential to prioritize your safety. After all, you wouldn't want your urbex adventure to turn into a real-life thriller! Here are some tips to keep in mind:

1. Never explore alone: The buddy system isn't just for kindergarteners. Exploring with a friend can keep you safe in case of an emergency and provide an extra set of eyes for spotting potential hazards.
2. Wear proper attire: Dress for success (and safety) by donning sturdy shoes, long sleeves, and pants to protect against scrapes and stumbles.
3. Be mindful of your surroundings: Keep an eye out for hazards like crumbling floors, broken glass, and rusty nails. Slow and steady wins the urbex race!

The Art of Capturing the Beauty in Decay
As an urban explorer, your mission is to reveal the hidden beauty of abandoned spaces. To do so, consider these artistic elements:

1. Composition: Think outside the (crumbling) box by trying unconventional angles and framing. Capture the essence of the space by incorporating its natural lines, shapes, and textures.
2. Light: Natural light can transform an abandoned building into a breathtaking work of art. Experiment with the interplay of light and shadows to create moody, evocative images.
3. Storytelling: Each abandoned space has a story to tell. Unearth its narrative by focusing on the details – an old chair, a broken window, or a forgotten toy. These relics of the past can speak volumes.

Putting the "Fun" in Fungi: Photographing Nature's Takeover

One of the most mesmerizing aspects of abandoned spaces is how nature reclaims them. Plants, fungi, and wildlife slowly take over, creating an enchanting fusion of the natural and the man-made. Embrace this fascinating juxtaposition by:

1. Capturing contrasts: Highlight the contrast between the industrial and the organic, such as ivy creeping over a rusty railing or a tree sprouting through a cracked floor.
2. Focusing on flora and fauna: Showcase the resilience of nature by documenting the plants and animals that have made the abandoned space their home.

Leaving No Trace: The Urbex Code of Conduct

As an urban explorer, you're an ambassador for this unique art form. It's crucial to respect the spaces you visit and leave them as you found them. Remember, take only photographs and leave only footprints.

And there you have it, intrepid explorer! By embracing the spirit of adventure and following these tips, you'll be on your way to creating captivating images that celebrate the hidden beauty of abandoned spaces. So strap on your camera bag, lace up your boots, and set out on your own urban exploration odyssey. The world awaits!

Camera Settings

To capture the essence of abandoned spaces in your urban exploration photography, consider the following camera settings as a starting point. Keep in mind that settings will vary based on the specific conditions, available light, and desired outcome for each shot:

1. Shooting Mode: Aperture Priority (A or Av) or Manual (M) mode will give you the most control over depth of field and exposure. Use Aperture Priority for quicker adjustments, or Manual mode for full control.
2. Aperture: To emphasize the depth and detail in your scene, use a mid-range aperture like f/8 or f/11. If you're aiming for a shallow depth of field to isolate a specific subject, consider using a wider aperture, such as f/2.8 or f/4.
3. Shutter Speed: Depending on your aperture and ISO settings, you may need to adjust the shutter speed to achieve a well-exposed image. In low-light conditions, use a slower shutter speed (e.g., 1/30s or 1/15s), but be mindful of potential camera shake. A tripod can help you avoid blurry images at slower shutter speeds.
4. ISO: Start with a low ISO setting (100-400) to minimize noise in your images. In darker environments, you may need to increase the ISO to achieve proper exposure. Be cautious of higher ISO settings, as they can introduce noise and compromise image quality.

5. White Balance: Set your white balance to "Auto" or choose a specific setting based on the available light (e.g., "Shade" or "Cloudy" for overcast days). You can also fine-tune the white balance in post-processing if you shoot in RAW format.

6. Focus: Use manual focus or single-point autofocus to ensure sharpness on your desired subject. In low-light situations, manual focus might be more reliable.

7. Image Stabilization: If your camera or lens has image stabilization, enable it to minimize camera shake, especially when shooting handheld at slower shutter speeds.

8. Bracketing: In high-contrast environments, consider using exposure bracketing to capture multiple exposures of the same scene. You can then blend these exposures in post-processing to create a single, well-balanced image.

9. File Format: Shoot in RAW format for maximum flexibility in post-processing. RAW files retain more information, allowing you to make adjustments without losing image quality.

51. A unique sculpture or installation art

A Symphony of Sculptures: Capturing the Magic of Installation Art

Picture yourself meandering through an enchanting art exhibition, where the vibrant colors, dynamic shapes, and intricate details of a breathtaking sculpture or installation demand to be immortalized. As a photography enthusiast, how could you possibly resist the urge to whip out your trusty lens and capture the magic?
Fear not, my friends, for I am here to guide you on this visually thrilling journey!

First, let's delve into the importance of planning your photographic escapade. If you're visiting an exhibit, museum, or public installation, be sure to check the rules regarding photography. While many venues encourage visitors to snap away, others may have strict guidelines to follow. So, remember the age-old adage: "When in Rome, do as the Romans do," or in our case, "When in the gallery, do as the gallery says."

With permissions in place, let's discuss the art of composing your masterpiece. You'll want to consider the context of the sculpture or installation. Is it situated in a serene garden or bustling cityscape? Use the environment to your advantage! A harmonious blend of subject and background can elevate your photo to the realm of the extraordinary. But be cautious: a cluttered backdrop can steal the limelight from your show-stopping subject, and nobody wants that, now do they?

When it comes to angles, the world is your oyster! Break free from the shackles of routine, and experiment with different perspectives. Get low, get high—heck, even get sideways if that's what tickles your fancy! Unconventional angles can reveal hidden dimensions and breathe new life into your subject. As the wise photographer once said, "Variety is the spice of life, and the secret sauce of photography."

Ah, now comes the all-important question of lighting. Whether you're blessed with the sun's natural glow or grappling with the temperamental nature of indoor lighting, understanding your light source is crucial. Soft, diffused light is the holy grail for capturing the subtleties of a sculpture's form and texture.
But don't shy away from shadows! They can add drama, depth, and intrigue to your composition. The interplay of light and shadow is an art unto itself—embrace it, and watch your photography soar!

Now, let's talk about the pièce de résistance: post-processing. In the digital age, photo editing is a veritable playground for photographers, allowing you to fine-tune your images and truly make them your own. Whether you prefer the subtle touch of color correction or the transformative power of filters, post-processing can be the cherry on top of your photographic sundae.

One last pro tip: don't forget to enjoy the experience! It's easy to get caught up in the technicalities of photography, but remember, you're capturing a unique moment in time. So, take a step back, soak in the beauty of the sculpture or installation art, and let your passion for photography shine through.

Immortalizing the magic of sculptures and installation art is a thrilling and rewarding endeavor for photographers of all skill levels. By embracing experimentation, understanding your environment, and harnessing the power of post-processing, you can create stunning images that celebrate the beauty of the world's most captivating art forms.

Now, it's time to put these tips into practice and let your creative spirit run wild. And remember, the only bad photo is the one you didn't take!

Camera Settings

While there's no one-size-fits-all solution for capturing the perfect shot of a sculpture or installation art, these general camera settings will help you get started:

1. Aperture: Set your aperture between f/4 and f/11, depending on your desired depth of field. A wider

aperture (lower f-number) will create a shallow depth of field, isolating the subject from the background, while a narrower aperture (higher f-number) will increase the depth of field, keeping more of the scene in focus.

2. Shutter Speed: Choose a shutter speed that complements the lighting conditions and your subject. If you're working in low light or capturing a moving installation, a slower shutter speed (1/30s to 1/60s) may be necessary. For well-lit subjects or handheld shots, opt for a faster shutter speed (1/125s or higher) to avoid camera shake and motion blur.

3. ISO: Keep your ISO as low as possible (100-400) to minimize noise and maintain image quality. If you're shooting in low light or with a fast shutter speed, you may need to increase your ISO (800-1600) to compensate for the lack of light. Be mindful of noise levels, and adjust accordingly.

4. White Balance: Set your white balance to match the lighting conditions, ensuring that the colors in your image are accurate. Auto white balance (AWB) is a good starting point, but you may need to fine-tune using presets (such as daylight, cloudy, or tungsten) or by manually adjusting the color temperature.

5. Focus Mode: Use single-shot autofocus (AF-S or One-Shot) for stationary subjects and continuous autofocus (AF-C or AI Servo) for moving installations. Don't forget to experiment with manual focus to achieve precise control over your focal point.

6. Metering Mode: Choose a metering mode that best suits your scene. Evaluative or matrix metering is ideal for evenly lit subjects, while spot or center-weighted metering is recommended for challenging lighting conditions or when the subject is dramatically lit.

7. Image Format: Shoot in RAW format to retain the maximum amount of detail and have greater flexibility during post-processing. If your camera doesn't support RAW or you prefer not to edit your images, choose the highest-quality JPEG setting available.

Adjust the settings based on your specific environment and subject, and ultimately find the perfect balance to capture the magic of the sculpture or installation art before you.

52. A moment of joy or laughter

Capturing a Slice of Happiness: Photographing Joy and Laughter

You're at a gathering with family and friends, the atmosphere is brimming with love and laughter, and suddenly, someone cracks a joke that sends everyone into fits of giggles. Wouldn't you want to freeze that moment, preserve it like a precious gem?

Say no more, dear photography enthusiast! Today, we're delving into the delightful world of photographing joy and laughter, and how to do it with panache.

First and foremost, let's address the elephant in the room - the art of candid photography. Capturing genuine expressions of happiness is much like trying to catch a butterfly in your hands; it's elusive, fleeting, and oh-so-delicate. So, the trick lies in being inconspicuous and patient.

Blend into the background, and let the moments unfold naturally. Remember, a photographer is like a ninja – unseen, unheard, and unbelievably skilled at snapping those precious moments. Next, keep your eyes peeled for the "golden moments." They're those split seconds when the stars align, and you witness a genuine smile, a hearty laugh, or a tender hug. The beauty of these moments is that they're unscripted and unrehearsed – and that's what makes them priceless. So, whether you're at a birthday party or a backyard barbecue, always have your trusty camera at the ready. It's like being a happiness hunter, seeking out those moments that make hearts swell and spirits soar.

Now, let's talk about the technical side of things. When photographing joy and laughter, you'll want to use a fast shutter speed to freeze the action. This will ensure your subjects are in focus, and you won't end up with blurry, mid-laugh snapshots. Don't be afraid to bump up the ISO if needed, as a little noise is far better than a missed moment. Remember, it's not about perfection; it's about preserving that pure, unfiltered joy.

Another key aspect is composition. When framing your shots, consider the rule of thirds and position your subjects accordingly. This will create visual balance and add depth to your photographs. Also, experiment with different angles to give your images a unique perspective.
Try shooting from a low angle for that larger-than-life feel or opt for a bird's-eye view to showcase the infectious energy of a group laugh. The world is your playground, and your camera is your paintbrush – so let your creativity run wild!

Lastly, don't forget the power of post-processing. A little touch-up can go a long way in enhancing your photographs. Adjust the brightness, contrast, and saturation levels to make those smiles shine even brighter.

Just be mindful not to overdo it, as you don't want to compromise the authenticity of the moment. After all, you're not looking to create caricatures but rather, to immortalize the essence of joy and laughter.

So all in all, photographing moments of joy and laughter is an art form that transcends technical prowess. It's about embracing the beauty of genuine emotion, and capturing those fleeting instances that warm our hearts and make life worth living. So, next time you find yourself in a room full of love and laughter, remember these tips and get ready to seize the day, one glorious snapshot at a time. Happy clicking!

Camera Settings

While there's no one-size-fits-all approach to camera settings, certain adjustments can help you achieve stunning results when photographing joy and laughter. Here are some recommended settings to start with:

1. Shutter Speed: To capture the spontaneity of laughter and freeze the action, opt for a fast shutter speed. Consider using at least 1/250s or even faster, such as 1/500s or 1/1000s, depending on the intensity of the movement.
2. Aperture: To ensure your subject is in focus while maintaining a pleasant background blur, choose a medium aperture, such as f/4 or f/5.6. If you want

to capture more detail in the background or shoot a larger group, opt for a narrower aperture like f/8 or f/11.

3. ISO: Set your ISO according to the lighting conditions. In well-lit environments, keep your ISO low, around 100-200. In low-light situations, you may need to increase it to 800 or even 1600. Keep in mind that higher ISOs can introduce noise into your images, so only increase the ISO when necessary.

4. Focus Mode: Select continuous autofocus (AF-C) or AI Servo (Canon) to track moving subjects and maintain sharp focus on their expressions.

5. Drive Mode: Choose continuous shooting or burst mode to capture multiple frames in quick succession. This increases your chances of capturing the perfect moment.

6. Metering Mode: Use matrix (Nikon) or evaluative (Canon) metering to ensure balanced exposure throughout the scene. Alternatively, you can use spot metering if you want to expose specifically for your subject's face.

7. White Balance: Adjust the white balance based on the lighting conditions (e.g., daylight, shade, or tungsten) to achieve accurate colors. Alternatively, you can set the white balance to auto and make adjustments in post-processing if needed.

Trial and error – that's how you'll grow as a photographer and capture those magical moments.

Conclusion

In the magical world of photography, the possibilities are endless, and the journey is exhilarating. Armed with a camera and a little imagination, you have the power to create, preserve, and share memories, stories, and emotions in a way that transcends time and space.

It has been a pleasure to guide you through 52 fabulous photography ideas that have been designed to unleash your inner artist and transform the way you see the world around you.

As we reach the conclusion of this photographic odyssey, it is essential to remember that photography is about much more than snapping pictures. It is an art form, a means of communication, and a window into the soul. Photography allows us to explore our environment, express our individuality, and forge connections with others. So, don't be shy! Embrace your unique perspective and let your creativity run wild.

Throughout our journey, we have dabbled in various photography genres and techniques, from the elegance of black and white portraits to the enchanting realm of macro photography. We have experimented with long exposures, played with lighting, and ventured into the world of abstract photography, all while marveling at the beauty and diversity of our surroundings.

Remember, the key to photography is to keep learning and growing, so don't be afraid to step out of your comfort zone and try new things. The world is your canvas, and your camera is the paintbrush – let your imagination be your guide. There is a saying that I absolutely agree with:

"The only bad photograph is the one you didn't take."

 So, take a chance, take the plunge, and let your creativity run free!

As you continue your photographic journey, remember to stay curious and observant. The world is brimming with untold stories and hidden gems, waiting to be discovered and captured through the lens of your camera. Keep your eyes open, your mind receptive, and your heart engaged – for the best photographs are not merely images, but emotions and experiences distilled into visual form.

In the end, photography is about sharing your unique perspective with the world and forging a connection with your audience. So, keep clicking, keep experimenting, and keep creating memories that will last a lifetime.

Remember, every picture tells a story – and the world is waiting to hear yours.

So, dear reader, it's time to take your camera, explore the world, and make some magic happen. Who knows, the next Ansel Adams, Annie Leibovitz, or Steve McCurry might just be you!

As we bid adieu to this delightful journey, let your passion for photography flourish and your creativity soar. And always remember, in the realm of photography, the only limit is your imagination.

Onwards and upwards, my fellow photographers! The world is your oyster, and there's no time like the present to start making a splash.

Stay safe and well, dear friends.

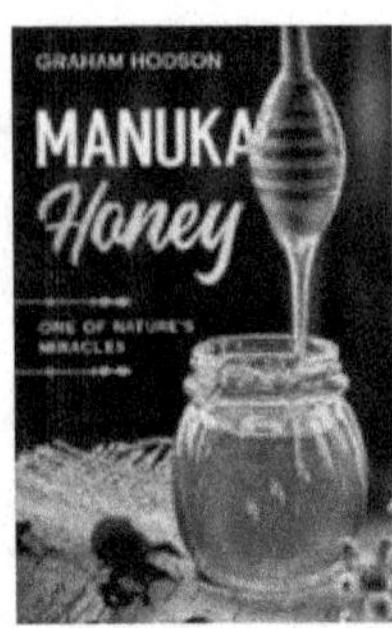

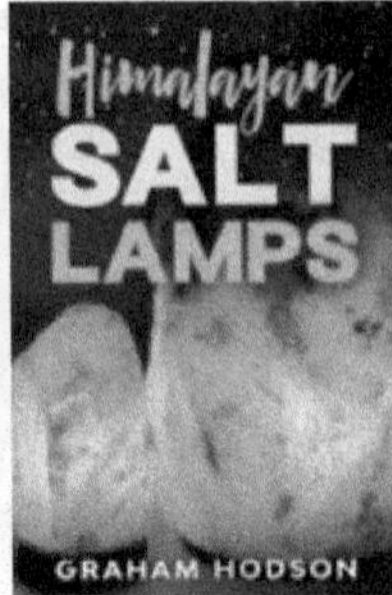

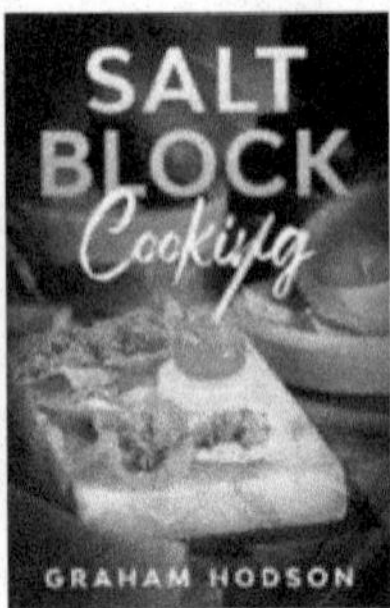

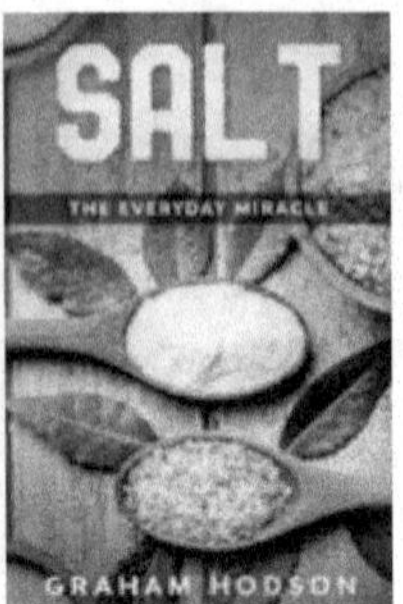

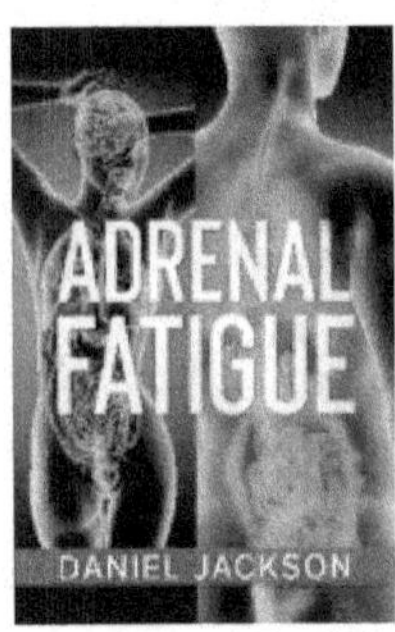

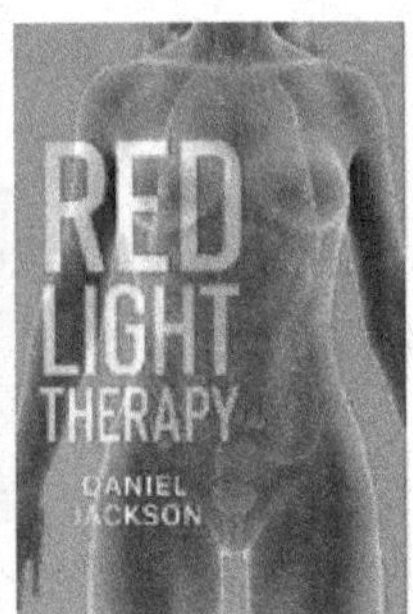

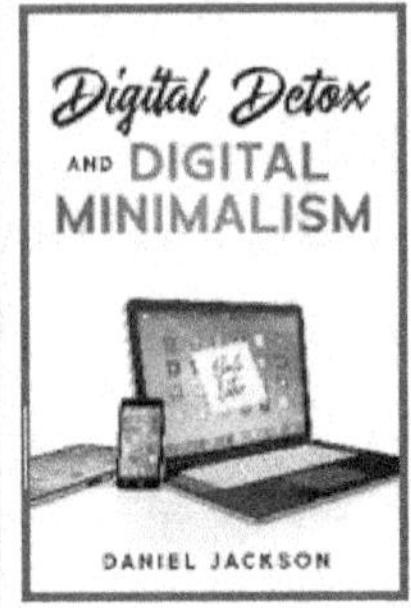

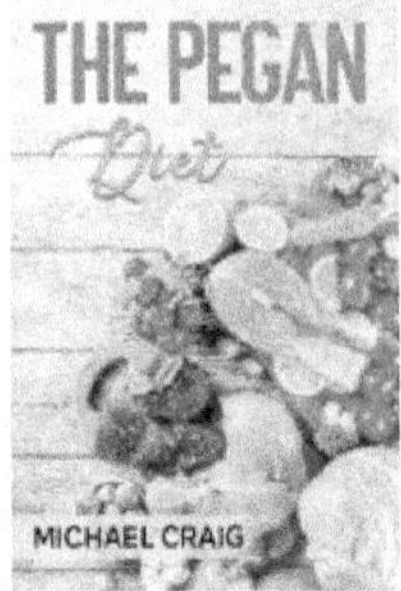

Take a look at more great books available from
Rockwood Publishing

... some for FREE!

Just visit the link below:

rockwoodpublishing.co.uk

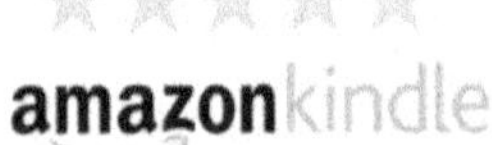

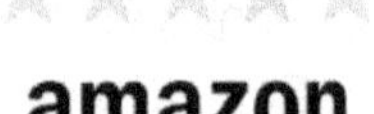

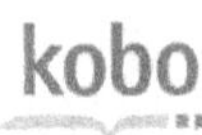

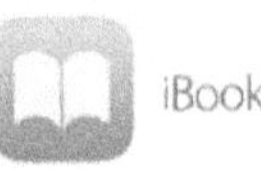

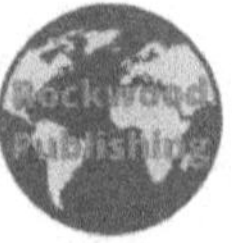

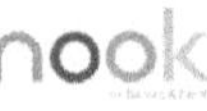

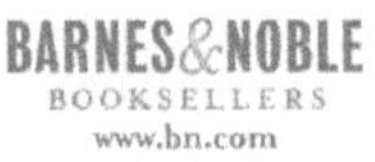

websites listed in this book. The inclusion of any website links does not necessarily imply a recommendation or endorse the views expressed within them. Rockwood Publishing takes no responsibility for, and will not be liable for, the websites being temporarily unavailable or being removed from the Internet. The accuracy and completeness of information provided herein and opinions stated herein are not guaranteed or warranted to produce any particular results, and the advice and strategies contained herein may not be suitable for every individual. The author shall not be liable for any loss incurred as a consequence of the use and application, directly or indirectly, of any information presented in this work. This publication is designed to provide information in regards to the subject matter covered. The information included in this book has been compiled to give an overview of the subject(s) and detail some of the symptoms, treatments etc. that are available to people with this condition. It is not intended to give medical advice. For a firm diagnosis of your condition, and for a treatment plan suitable for you, you should consult your doctor or consultant. The writer of this book and the publisher are not responsible for any damages or negative consequences following any of the treatments or methods highlighted in this book. Website links are for informational purposes and should not be seen as a personal endorsement; the same applies to the products detailed in this book. The reader should also be aware that although the web links included were correct at the time of writing, they may become out of date in the future.

Disclaimers

The content contained within this book is for information and entertainment purposes only, and in no way purports to represent professional medical opinion. It should NOT be used as a substitute for expert advice, and you must consult with your designated health professional before acting upon any information contained herein or before undertaking any practice whose methodology is referred to in this book. The author is NOT a registered health professional and the text merely represents personal opinion, not medical fact. The author cannot be held responsible for the consequences of any action derived from the reading of this book, as the content is not based on diagnosis and subsequent regimen. It is the reader's responsibility to seek proper, professional medical advice from a registered health practitioner in connection with any material contained within this book.

Legal Disclaimer (part 1)

Nothing in this book should be construed as an attempt to diagnose, treat or cure. The information in this book is intended to be a community resource. The author takes no responsibility for any informational material or brochures produced using information taken from this book. The author has endeavoured to ensure that all information is correct at the time of publication. This information, however, is subject to change without notice. The author makes no warranty with regard to the accuracy of any

information and will not be liable for any errors or omissions. Any liability that arises as a result of this information is hereby excluded to the fullest extent allowed by law.
This information should not be used as a substitute for seeking independent professional advice.

Legal Disclaimer (part 2)

Disclaimer and Terms of Use:

a) i. In publishing this information, the author makes no representations concerning the efficacy, appropriateness or suitability of any products or treatments. Use this information at your own risk. The compiler is not a doctor and has no medical background or training.

ii. Statements and information regarding dietary supplements, books and any products mentioned have not been evaluated by any health authority and are not intended to diagnose, treat, cure or prevent any disease or health condition.

b) In view of the possibility of human error, neither the author nor any other party involved in providing this information, warrant that the information contained therein is in every respect accurate or complete and they are not responsible nor liable for any errors or omissions that may be found or for the results obtained from the use of such information. The entire risk as to use of this information is assumed by the user.

c) You are encouraged to consult other sources and confirm the information.

d) The information you access is provided "as is". No warranty, expressed or implied, is given as to the accuracy, completeness or timeliness of any information herein, or for obtaining legal advice. To the fullest extent permissible pursuant to applicable law, neither the author nor any other parties who have been involved in the creation, preparation, printing, or delivering of this information assume responsibility for the completeness, accuracy, timeliness, errors or omissions of said information and assume no liability for any direct, incidental, consequential, indirect, or punitive damages as well as any circumstance for any complication, injuries, side effects or other medical accidents to person or property arising from or in connection with the use or reliance upon any information contained herein.

e) The author is not responsible for the contents of any linked site or any link contained in a linked site, or any changes or update to such sites. The inclusion of any link does not imply endorsement by the author. The author makes no representations or claims as to the quality, content and accuracy of the information, services, products, messages which may be provided by such resources, and specifically disclaims any warranties, including but not limited to implied or express warranties of merchantability or fitness for any particular usage, application or purpose.

f) The information provided is general in nature and is intended for educational and informational purposes only. It is not intended to replace or substitute the evaluation, judgment, diagnosis, and medical or preventative care of a physician, paediatrician, therapist and/or health care provider.

g) Any medical, nutritional, dietetic, therapeutic or other decisions, dosages, treatments or drug regimes should be made in consultation with a health care practitioner. Do not discontinue treatment or medication without first consulting your physician, clinician or therapist.

h) By reading this information, you signify your assent to these terms and conditions of use. If you do not agree to these terms and conditions of use, do not read/use this information. If any provision of these terms and conditions of use shall be determined to be unlawful, void or for any reason unenforceable, then that provision shall be deemed severable from this agreement and shall not affect the validity and enforceability of any remaining provisions.

i) The information, services, products, messages and other materials, individually and collectively, are provided with the understanding that the author is not engaged in rendering medical advice or recommendations.

j) The information and the terms of use are subject to change without notice. The material provided as is without warranty of any kind and may include inaccuracies and/or typographical errors. The author makes no representations about the suitability of this information for any purpose. The author disclaims all warranties with regard to this information, including all implied warranties, and in no event shall the author be held liable, resulting from, or in any way related to, the use of this information.

k) The unauthorized alteration of the content of this information is expressly prohibited. The author, its agents and representatives shall not be responsible for any claims, actions or damages which may arise on account of the unauthorized alteration of this information.